D0904750

REF. J912 P834C
Porter, Malcolm.
Children's atlas of the
world   DEC 2 0 2006

MID-CONTINENT PUBLIC LIBRARY
Riverside Branch
2700 N.W. Vivion Road   **RS**
Riverside, MO 64150

WITHDRAWN
FROM THE RECORDS OF THE
MID-CONTINENT PUBLIC LIBRARY

CHILDREN'S Atlas OF THE WORLD

GARETH**STEVENS**
PUBLISHING
A Member of the WRC Media Family of Companies

CHILDREN'S Atlas OF THE WORLD

Malcolm Porter

GARETH**STEVENS**

GS

PUBLISHING

A Member of the WRC Media Family of Companies

MID-CONTINENT PUBLIC LIBRARY - BTM

3 0003 00252897 2

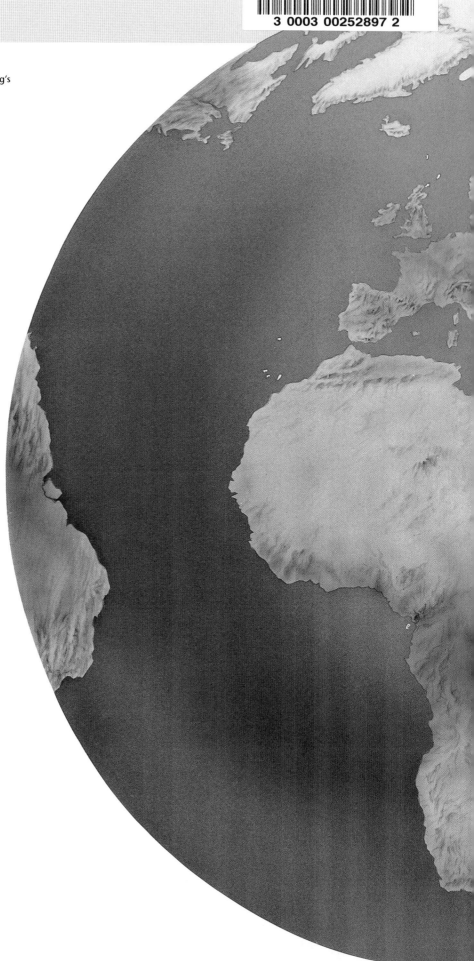

Please visit our web site at: www.garethstevens.com
For a free color catalog describing Gareth Stevens Publishing's
list of high-quality books and multimedia programs, call
1-800-542-2595 (USA) or 1-800-387-3178 (Canada).
Gareth Stevens Publishing's fax: (414) 332-3567.

Library of Congress Cataloging-in-Publication Data

Porter, Malcolm.
      Children's atlas of the world / Malcolm Porter.
          p. cm.
      Includes index.
      ISBN 0-8368-4989-2 (lib. bdg.)
      1. Children's atlases.   I. Title.
   G1021.P6   2005
   912—dc22   2005045000

This edition first published in 2006 by
Gareth Stevens Publishing
A Member of the WRC Media Family of Companies
330 West Olive Street, Suite 100
Milwaukee, WI 53212 USA

This revised and updated edition first published by
Evans Brothers Limited 2004,
2A Portman Mansions, Chiltern Street,
London W1U 6NR, United Kingdom.
Copyright © Malcom Porter and A S Publishing 2004

This U.S. edition © copyright 2006 by Gareth Stevens, Inc.,
and published under license from Evans Brothers Limited.

A S Publishing consultant editor: Keith Lye
A S Publishing assistant editor: Paul Dempsey
Gareth Stevens editor: Betsy Rasmussen
Gareth Stevens cover design: Scott M. Krall

All rights reserved. No part of this book may be
reproduced, stored in a retrieval system, or transmitted
in any form or by any means, electronic, mechanical,
photocopying, recording, or otherwise, without the
prior written permission of the copyright holder.

Printed in the United States of America

1 2 3 4 5 6 7 8 9 09 08 07 06 05

MID-CONTINENT PUBLIC LIBRARY
Riverside Branch
2700 N.W. Vivion Road
Riverside, MO 64150

RS

CONTENTS

Planet Earth

Our Earth is one of the nine planets that circle the Sun. It is the third planet from the Sun. Today, we can see photographs of the Earth taken from space. These show land areas, called continents, and blue seas and oceans.

Maps show the same things, but they give much more information than space photographs. They show the names and positions of cities and towns, and other features such as rivers and mountains.

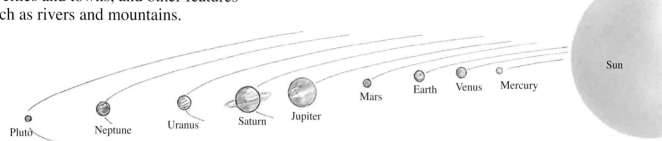

As the Earth circles the Sun, it spins on its axis, an imaginary line joining the North Pole, the center of the Earth, and the South Pole.

Some lines appear on maps. One line around the middle of the Earth, exactly halfway between the North and South Poles, is called the equator. Other lines are called the Tropic of Cancer, in the northern half of the world, and the Tropic of Capricorn, in the southern half. Two important lines go around the cold areas near the poles. They are the Arctic and Antarctic Circles.

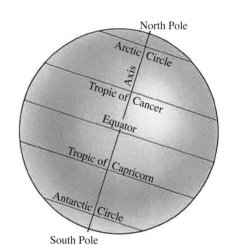

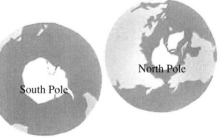

Land Areas			
	Area (sq miles)	Area (sq km)	2004 Population
North America	8,260,174	21,393,762	508,915,797
South America	6,765,422	17,522,371	366,803,836
Europe*	8,813,128	5,830,105	585,607,035
Russia	6,560,379	16,995,800	143,782,338
Asia*	11,979,676	31,027,230	3,866,437,804
Africa	11,507,789	29,805,048	873,742,214
Australia and Oceania	3,254,339	8,428,702	32,352,618
Antarctica	5,405,428	14,000,000	31,000

*Excluding Russia

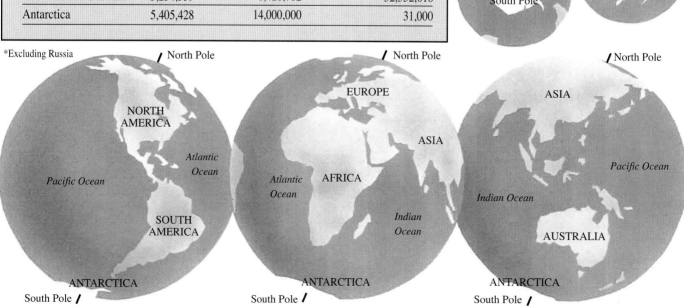

World Records

Mountains
The highest mountains in five continents are shown on the right. The world's highest peak is Mount Everest.

Aconcagua
(SOUTH AMERICA)
22,834 feet
(6,959 m)

McKinley
(NORTH AMERICA)
20,320 feet
(6,194 m)

Everest
(ASIA)
29,035 feet
(8,850 m)

Kilimanjaro
(AFRICA)
19,340 feet
(5,895 m)

Elbrus
(EUROPE)
18,510 feet
(5,642 m)

Rivers
The longest rivers in the world are shown on the right. The Nile in Africa is the longest.

Volga (EUROPE) 2,290 miles (3,685 km)

Murray-Darling (AUSTRALIA) 2,310 miles (3,717 km)

Mississippi (NORTH AMERICA) 2,340 miles (3,765 km)

Chang Jiang (ASIA) 3,964 miles (6,378 km)

Amazon (SOUTH AMERICA) 4,000 miles (6,436 km)

Nile (AFRICA) 4,160 miles (6,693 km)

Deserts
Deserts cover about one-seventh of the world's land areas. The Sahara in North Africa is the largest.

Sahara (AFRICA) 3,500,000 sq miles (9,065,000 sq km)

Great Victoria Desert (AUSTRALIA) 150,000 sq miles (388,500 sq km)

Rub al Khali (ASIA) 250,000 sq miles (647,5000 sq km)

Gobi Desert (ASIA) 500,000 sq miles (1,295,000 sq km)

Kalahari Desert (AFRICA) 225,000 sq miles (582,750 sq km)

Lakes
The world's largest lake is the Caspian Sea, so called because its water is salty. The largest freshwater lake is Lake Superior.

Lake Superior
(NORTH AMERICA)
31,700 sq miles
(82,100 sq km)

Lake Huron
(NORTH AMERICA)
23,000 sq miles
(59,570 sq km)

Aral Sea
(ASIA)
13,000 sq miles
(33,670 sq km)

Caspian Sea
(ASIA/EUROPE)
143,000 sq miles
(371,000 sq km)

Lake Michigan
(NORTH AMERICA)
22,300 sq miles
(57,750 sq km)

Lake Victoria
(AFRICA)
26,800 sq miles
(69,500 sq km)

Islands
Islands are land areas surrounded by water. The world's largest island, Greenland, is mostly covered by ice.

New Guinea
(AUSTRALIA and OCEANIA)
306,000 sq miles
(792,540 sq km)

Baffin Island
(NORTH AMERICA)
195,928 sq miles
(507,528 sq km)

Greenland
(NORTH AMERICA)
840,000 sq miles
(2,175,000 sq km)

Borneo
(ASIA)
280,000 sq miles
(725,450 sq km)

Madagascar
(AFRICA)
226,658 sq miles
(587,040 sq km)

Deeps and Depressions
The deepest point on land is the shore of the Dead Sea in Israel and Jordan. The deepest part of the oceans is in the Marianas Trench, in the Pacific.

Lowest point on land
Dead Sea shoreline (ASIA)
1,348 feet (411 m) below sea level

Deepest point in the oceans
Marianas Trench (PACIFIC OCEAN)
35,840 feet (10,924 m)

Deepest lake
Lake Baykal (ASIA)
5,315 feet (1,620 m) deep
or 3,822 feet (1,165 m)

Measuring Earth

Models of the Earth are called globes. The surfaces of globes are marked with networks of lines.

Some lines run around the globe. They are called lines of latitude, or parallels. The equator, the Tropics of Cancer and Capricorn, and the Arctic and Antarctic Circles are all lines of latitude.

Other lines on globes run at right angles to the lines of latitude, through both the North and South Poles. These are lines of longitude, or meridians.

Lines of latitude and longitude are marked on maps, which show the globe, or parts of it, on flat pieces of paper. The position of every place on Earth has its own latitude and longitude.

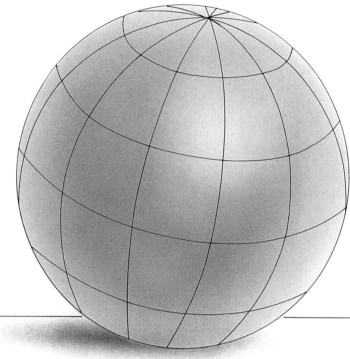

Latitude

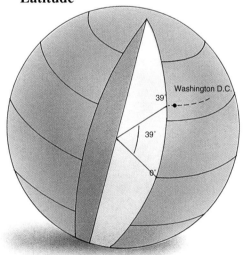

The latitude of the equator, which divides the Earth into two equal halves, called hemispheres, is 0 degrees. The latitude of the North Pole is 90 degrees North (90°N), while the latitude of the South Pole is 90 degrees South (90°S).

The latitude of places between the equator and the Poles is measured in degrees north or south of the equator. For example, the latitude of Washington, D.C., is nearly 39 degrees North. This means that the angle formed at the center of Earth between the equator and Washington, D.C., is nearly 39 degrees.

The Tropic of Cancer is latitude 23.5 degrees North, while the Tropic of Capricorn is 23.5 degrees South. The Arctic Circle is 66.5 degrees North, while the Antarctic Circle is 66.5 degrees South.

Longitude

Lines of longitude are measured 180 degrees east and west of the prime meridian, or 0 degrees longitude. The prime meridian runs through the North Pole, Greenwich, in London, England, and the South Pole. The line was established at an international conference in 1884.

Washington, D.C., for example, is situated at 77 degrees West. This means that the angle formed at the center of Earth between the prime meridian and another line of longitude running through Washington, D.C., is 77 degrees west of the prime meridian.

The 180 degree line of longitude east and west of the prime meridian runs through the Pacific Ocean, on the far side of the world from the prime meridian. The prime meridian and the 180 degree line of longitude divide Earth into two hemispheres, east and west, in the same way that the equator divides north and south.

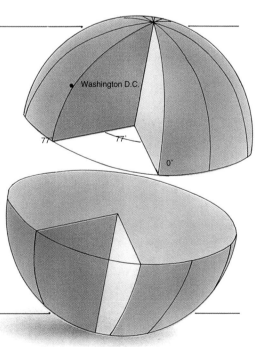

Map Projections

One of the problems faced by mapmakers is that it is impossible to show Earth on a flat piece of paper without distorting it to some extent. You can understand the problem if you imagine that the world is an orange. If you peel the orange, there is no way that you can stretch the peel flat without breaking it up and crushing the pieces.

Azimuthal projection

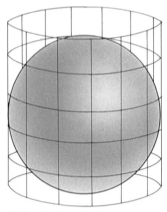

Cylindrical projection

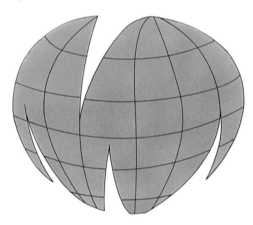

To solve this problem, mapmakers use map projections. Imagine a glass globe with the network of lines of latitude and longitude (called graticules) engraved on it. Put a light inside the globe and the graticules will be cast, or projected, onto a flat sheet of paper touching it at one point to produce an *azimuthal projection*. Imagine doing the same with a paper cylinder to produce a *cylindrical projection* or a paper cone to produce a *conical projection*.

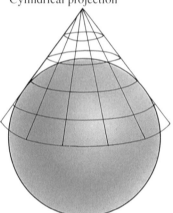

Conical projection

Projections in This Atlas

The projections shown above are called perspective projections. But, in practice, mapmakers seldom use these projections. Instead, they use projections that they develop using mathematics so that they can reproduce accurately areas, shapes, distances and directions. Projections used for maps of the world can preserve some of these features, although no single projection can show them all.

The maps that show the continent at the beginning of each chapter of this atlas have been specially drawn to show how the continent looks from space. The map on the right shows how Africa on page 69 would look with lines of latitude and longitude.

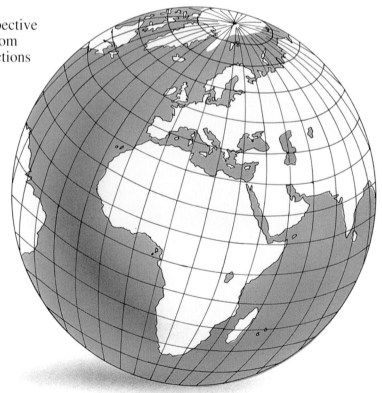

How to Use the Atlas

To put as much information as possible on a map, mapmakers use symbols. To get the most out of the maps in this atlas, it helps to know the symbols.

Cities with a population of more than 1 million people	**New York City** •
Cities with a population between 100,000 and 1 million	**Atlantic City** •
Towns with a population of below 100,000	Vineland •
Capital city	**Washington D.C.** ▣
State capital	★ Phoenix
Mountain with its height	△ Mt. McKinley 20,320 feet
Mountain range	**Catskill Mts**
Dam	⊢
Island	**Island**
Archaeological site	∴

River Canal Lake	*River* *Canal* *Lake*
Country name	**CANADA**
Province or state name	MARYLAND
State, province, or country border	——

Key to land coloring

Forest	
Crops	
Dry Grassland	
Desert	
Tundra	
Polar	

Maps in the Atlas
The atlas starts with views of the world as a whole. The physical map of the world on pages 12–13 shows the world's main land features, while the political map on pages 14–15 shows the countries into which the world is divided.

The atlas contains sections on North America, South America, Europe, Asia, Africa, and Australia. Each section has a map showing where the continent is situated on the globe and the countries it contains. Other maps show groups of countries (or states) in the continent.

If you want to know facts about a country, such as its population or area, look at the table alongside the map.

The last section of the atlas has maps of the oceans and the polar regions.

Populations
Many large cities, such as Boston, have metropolitan area populations (4,391,344) that are greater than the city figures (581,616). Such cities have larger dot sizes on the map to emphasize their importance.

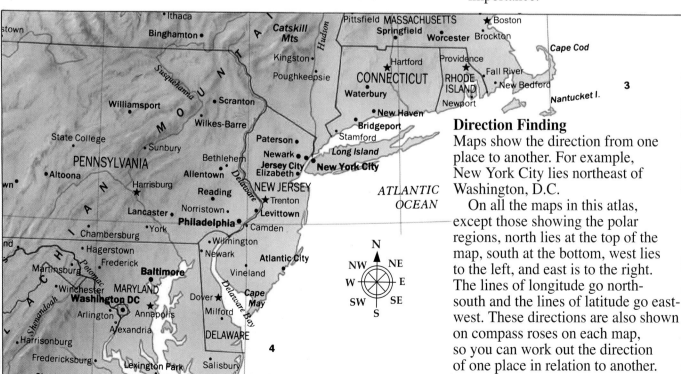

Direction Finding
Maps show the direction from one place to another. For example, New York City lies northeast of Washington, D.C.

On all the maps in this atlas, except those showing the polar regions, north lies at the top of the map, south at the bottom, west lies to the left, and east is to the right. The lines of longitude go north-south and the lines of latitude go east-west. These directions are also shown on compass roses on each map, so you can work out the direction of one place in relation to another.

Using the Index

To find a place in this atlas, use the index at the back of the book.

After each place name you will find a number and then a letter and a number. For example, if you want to find Rome, the capital of Italy, you will find the following entry in the index:

Rome 52 B3

You should then turn to page 52, where you will find the map of Italy and Southeastern Europe. Look for the square on the map labeled B at the top and 3 on the left-hand side. You will then find Rome in the square where B and 3 meet.

Scales and Distance

Maps are drawn to scale. This means that you can find the distance between places on a map.

The maps in this atlas have a scale line, marked in miles and kilometers. Place a piece of paper on this line, and mark off the distances shown. If you want to know the distance from San Diego to Lake Havasu City, place your piece of paper on the map with the zero end on San Diego. You will find that the distance to Lake Havasu City is about 200 miles (300 kilometers). See if you can find the distance between Cedar City and Flagstaff.

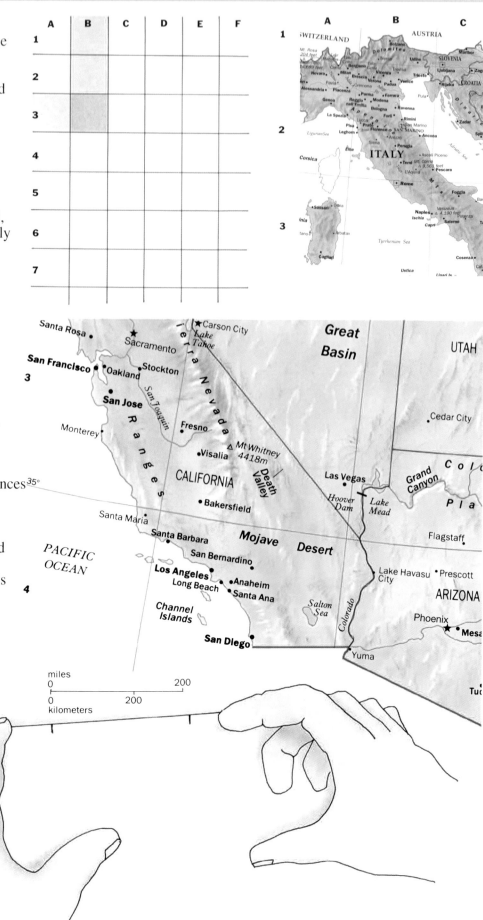

11

The Physical World

ARCTIC OCEAN

Baffin Island

Greenland

Arctic Circle

Mt. McKinley

Rocky Mts

Hudson Bay

Great Plains

Great Lakes

Appalachian Mts

NORTH AMERICA

Mississippi

Tropic of Cancer

Gulf of Mexico

West Indies

ATLANTIC OCEAN

Caribbean Sea

Equator

Amazon

Andes Mts

Selvas

SOUTH AMERICA

PACIFIC OCEAN

Tropic of Capricorn

Atacama Desert

Aconcagua

Tasman Sea

Patagonia

New Zealand

Antarctic Circle

ANTARCTICA

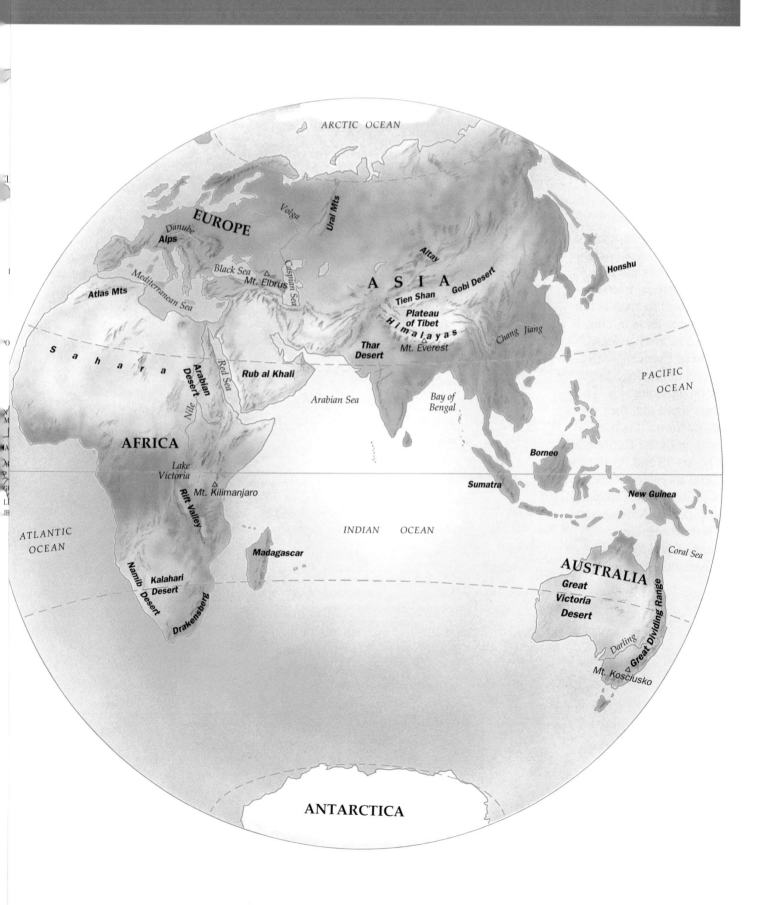

ARCTIC OCEAN

EUROPE

Volga

Ural Mts

Danube
Alps

Altay

A S I A

Gobi Desert

Honshu

Black Sea
△ Mt. Elbrus

Caspian Sea

Tien Shan

Atlas Mts

Mediterranean Sea

**Plateau
of Tibet**

H i m a l a y a s

Chang Jiang

**Thar
Desert**

△ Mt. Everest

S a h a r a

**Arabian
Desert**

Red Sea

Rub al Khali

Arabian Sea

*Bay of
Bengal*

PACIFIC
OCEAN

Nile

AFRICA

*Lake
Victoria*

Borneo

Sumatra

New Guinea

Rift Valley

△ Mt. Kilimanjaro

ATLANTIC
OCEAN

INDIAN   OCEAN

Madagascar

Coral Sea

AUSTRALIA

**Namib
Desert**

**Kalahari
Desert**

**Great
Victoria
Desert**

Great Dividing Range

Drakensberg

Darling

△ Mt. Kosciusko

ANTARCTICA

North America

North America, the fourth largest continent, contains the world's largest island, Greenland, and three huge countries: Canada, the United States, and Mexico. It also includes the smaller countries of Central America and the islands of the Caribbean.

The land of North America includes icy areas in the north and warm tropical places in the south. The United States contains both of North America's longest rivers, the Mississippi and Missouri Rivers, and the highest mountain, Mount McKinley in Alaska.

North America contains twenty-three independent countries. Its total population is about 509 million. Canada and the United States are rich, developed countries. But many people of Central America and the Caribbean are poor.

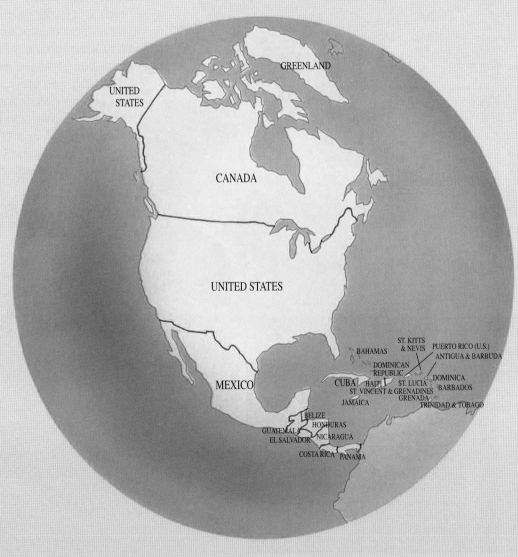

Canada and Greenland

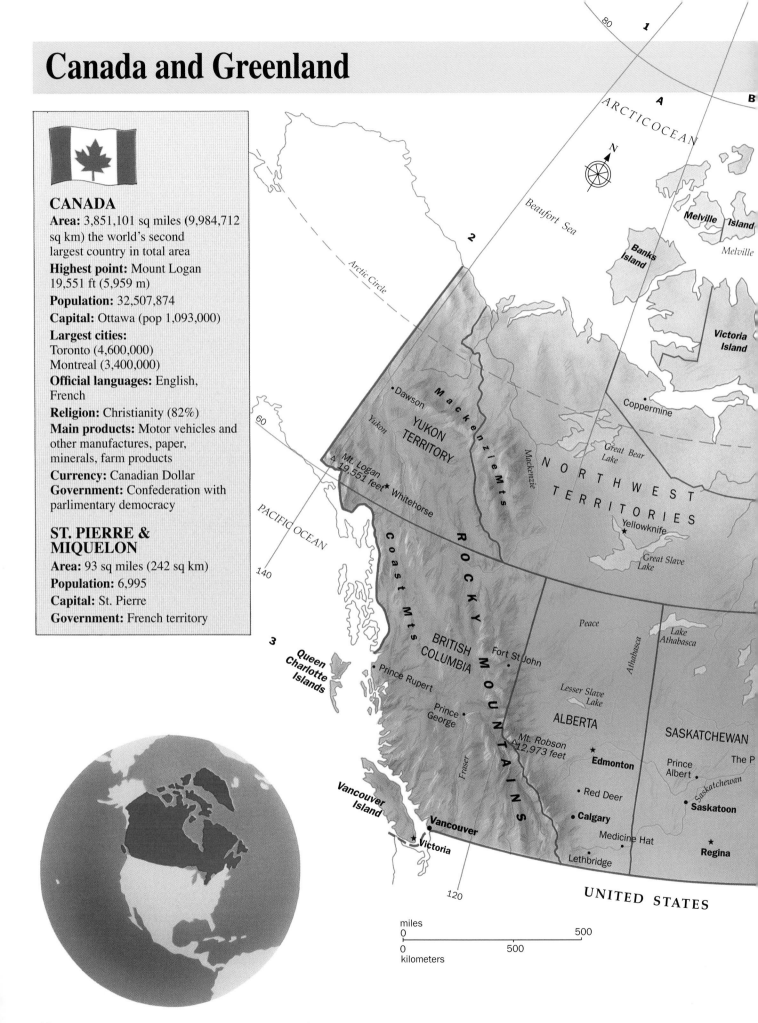

![Canadian flag]

CANADA

Area: 3,851,101 sq miles (9,984,712 sq km) the world's second largest country in total area

Highest point: Mount Logan 19,551 ft (5,959 m)

Population: 32,507,874

Capital: Ottawa (pop 1,093,000)

Largest cities:
Toronto (4,600,000)
Montreal (3,400,000)

Official languages: English, French

Religion: Christianity (82%)

Main products: Motor vehicles and other manufactures, paper, minerals, farm products

Currency: Canadian Dollar

Government: Confederation with parlimentary democracy

ST. PIERRE & MIQUELON

Area: 93 sq miles (242 sq km)

Population: 6,995

Capital: St. Pierre

Government: French territory

80
1
A
B

ARCTIC OCEAN

N

Beaufort Sea

Melville Island
Melville

Banks Island

Victoria Island

2

Arctic Circle

Mackenzie Mts

Dawson

Yukon

YUKON TERRITORY

Coppermine

Great Bear Lake

Mackenzie

N O R T H W E S T

60

Mt. Logan 19,551 feet
Whitehorse

Yellowknife

T E R R I T O R I E S

PACIFIC OCEAN

140

Coast Mts

R O C K Y

Great Slave Lake

3

Queen Charlotte Islands

BRITISH COLUMBIA

Prince Rupert

Fort St John

Peace

Lake Athabasca

Athabasca

M O U N T A I N S

Lesser Slave Lake

Prince George

Fraser

Mt. Robson 12,973 feet

ALBERTA

SASKATCHEWAN

The P

Vancouver Island

Edmonton

Prince Albert

Saskatchewan

Red Deer

Saskatoon

Vancouver

Calgary

Victoria

Medicine Hat

Regina

Lethbridge

120

UNITED STATES

miles
0   500
0   500
kilometers

C   D   E   F

Ellesmere
Island

Thule

Bathurst
Island

Devon Island

Baffin Bay

Disko
Island

GREENLAND
(DENMARK)

Gunnbjorn △
12,140 feet

Angmagssalik

Somerset
Island

Godhavn

Prince of
Wales
Island

Baffin
Island

Davis Strait

Frederikshaab

Cape
Farewell

King
William
Island

Melville
Peninsula

Godthab

40°

Southampton
Island

Iqaluit   Frobisher Bay

N U N A V U T

Hudson Strait

GREENLAND
Area: 836,330 sq miles
(2,166,095 sq km)
Population: 56,000
Capital: Godthab (pop 13,400)
Government: Self-governing part
of Denmark

Ungava
Peninsula

Nain

N E W F O U N D L A N D

Eskimo Point

LABRADOR

Hudson Bay

Churchill

St. John's

Churchill

James
Bay

Anticosti
Island

Corner
Brook

Newfoundland

ST. PIERRE &
MIQUELON
(FRANCE)

MANITOBA

Lake
Winnipeg

Fort
Albany

Fort Rupert

Q U E B E C

Chicoutimi

NEW
BRUNSWICK

Moncton

PRINCE
EDWARD ISLAND

Charlottetown

Glace Bay

Sydney

Lake
Manitoba

O N T A R I O

NOVA SCOTIA

Winnipeg   Kenora

Quebec

St. Lawrence

Fredericton

Saint John

Halifax

Brandon

Timmins

Trois-Rivières

Thunder Bay

Sudbury

Ottawa   Hull

Montreal

Cape Sable

60°

Sault Ste. Marie

Lake   Superior

Ottawa

ATLANTIC   OCEAN

0°

Peterborough

Kingston

Lake
Huron

Oshawa

Lake
Ontario

Kitchener

Toronto

Hamilton

Niagara Falls

London

Lake Erie

Lake
Michigan

Windsor

80°

United States

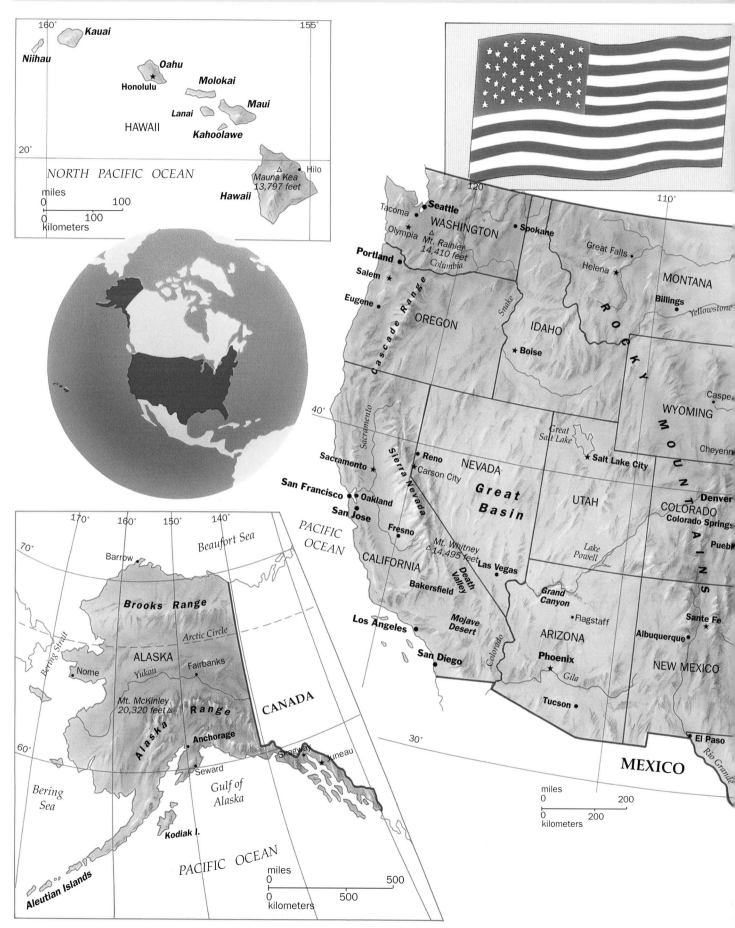

Kauai
160°
155°
Niihau
Oahu
Honolulu
Molokai
Maui
Lanai
Kahoolawe
HAWAII
20°

NORTH PACIFIC OCEAN
miles
0   100
0   100
kilometers

Hilo
Mauna Kea
13,797 feet
Hawaii

170°   160°   150°   140°
70°
Beaufort Sea
PACIFIC
OCEAN
Barrow
Brooks Range
Arctic Circle
Bering Strait
ALASKA
Fairbanks
Nome
Yukon
Mt. McKinley
20,320 feet
Range
Alaska
CANADA
Anchorage
60°
Skagway
Juneau
Seward
Bering
Sea
Gulf of
Alaska
Kodiak I.
Aleutian Islands
PACIFIC OCEAN
miles
0   500
0   500
kilometers

Tacoma   **Seattle**
120°
110°
WASHINGTON   • Spokane
Olympia   Mt. Rainier
14,410 feet
Great Falls
Portland
Columbia
Helena   ★
MONTANA
Salem
Billings   Yellowstone
Eugene
OREGON   Snake
IDAHO
Cascade Range
★ Boise
40°
Sacramento
Caspe
WYOMING
Great
Salt Lake
★ Salt Lake City
Cheyenn
Sierra Nevada
Reno
NEVADA
Sacramento
Carson City
San Francisco   Oakland
Great
Basin
UTAH
Denver
COLORADO
Colorado Springs
San Jose
Fresno
Lake
Powell
Mt. Whitney
14,495 feet
Las Vegas
Pueb
CALIFORNIA
Death
Valley
Bakersfield
Grand
Canyon
Santa Fe
Mojave
Desert
• Flagstaff
Los Angeles
Albuquerque
ARIZONA
Colorado
San Diego
Gila
NEW MEXICO
Phoenix
30°
Tucson •
El Paso
MEXICO
Rio Grande
miles
0   200
0   200
kilometers

20

UNITED STATES

Area: 3,718,709 sq miles (9,631,456 sq km); the world's third largest country in total area
Highest point: Mount McKinley, Alaska, 20,320 ft (6,194 m): the highest peak in North America
Population: 293,027,571

Capital: Washington, D.C. (pop 563,384)
Largest cities:
New York City (8,085,742)
Los Angeles (3,819,951)
Chicago (2,869,121)
Houston (2,009,690)
Philadelphia (1,479,339)
Principal language: English
Religion: Christianity (84%)

Economy: *Agriculture:* grains, crops, cattle, dairy products; *Mining:* coal, copper, gold, oil, iron, nickel, silver, uranium, zinc; *Industry:* machinery and transportation equipment, chemicals, food products
Currency: U.S. Dollar
Government: Federal republic

U.S. Northeastern States

 Kentucky

Area: 40,409 sq miles (104,659 sq km)
Population: 4,117,827
Capital: Frankfort (pop 27,408)
Largest city: Lexington (pop 266,798)

 West Virginia

Area: 24,230 sq miles (62,756 sq km)
Population: 1,810,354
Capital and largest city: Charleston (pop 51,394)

 Virginia

Area: 42,774 sq miles (110,785 sq km)
Population: 7,386,330
Capital: Richmond (pop 198,000)
Largest city: Virginia Beach (pop 439,467)

 Pennsylvania

Area: 46,055 sq miles (119,282 sq km)
Population: 12,365,455
Capital: Harrisburg (pop 48,322)
Largest city: Philadelphia (pop 1,479,339)

 New York

Area: 54,556 sq miles (141,300 sq km)
Population: 19,190,115
Capital: Albany (pop 93,919)
Largest city: New York City (pop 8,085,742) largest in the U.S.

 Vermont

Area: 9,614 sq miles (24,900 sq km)
Population: 619,107
Capital: Montpelier (pop 7,945)
Largest city: Burlington (pop 39,148)

 New Hampshire

Area: 9,350 sq miles (24,216 sq km)
Population: 1,287,687
Capital: Concord (pop 41,823)
Largest city: Manchester (pop 108,871)

 Maine

Area: 35,385 sq miles (91,647 sq km)
Population: 1,305,728
Capital: Augusta (pop 18,618)
Largest city: Portland (pop 63,635)

 Massachusetts

Area: 10,555 sq miles (27,337 sq km)
Population: 6,433,422
Capital and largest city: Boston (pop 581,616)

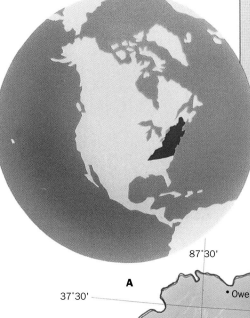

22

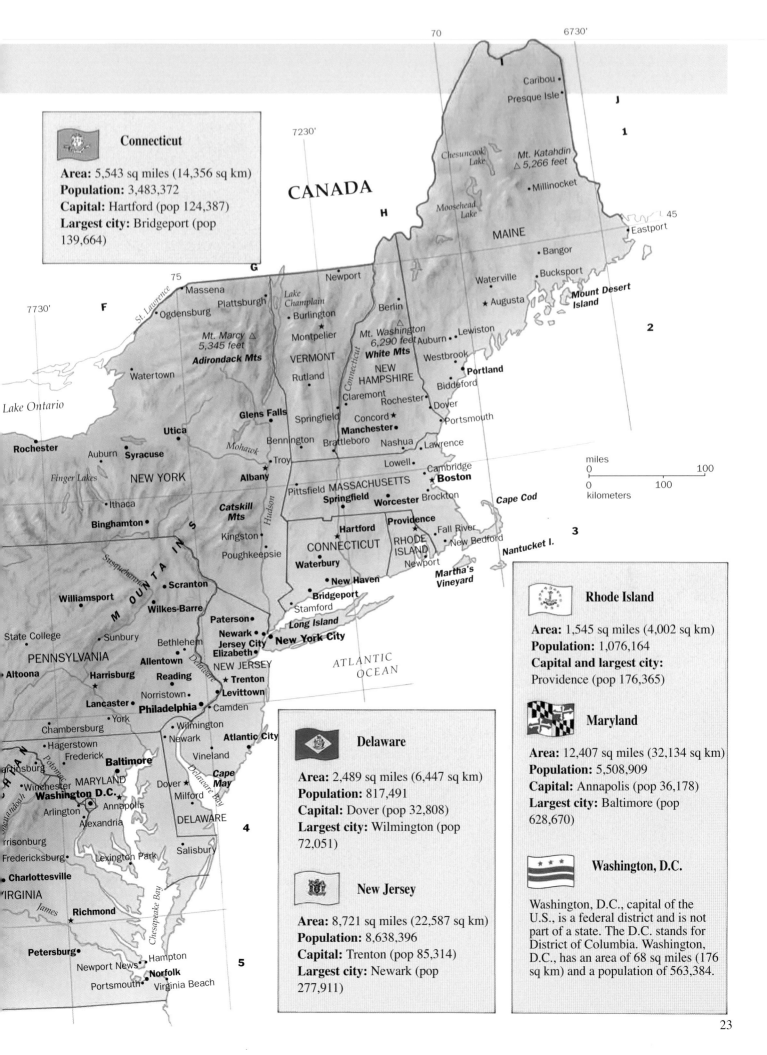

Connecticut

Area: 5,543 sq miles (14,356 sq km)
Population: 3,483,372
Capital: Hartford (pop 124,387)
Largest city: Bridgeport (pop 139,664)

Rhode Island

Area: 1,545 sq miles (4,002 sq km)
Population: 1,076,164
Capital and largest city: Providence (pop 176,365)

Maryland

Area: 12,407 sq miles (32,134 sq km)
Population: 5,508,909
Capital: Annapolis (pop 36,178)
Largest city: Baltimore (pop 628,670)

Washington, D.C.

Washington, D.C., capital of the U.S., is a federal district and is not part of a state. The D.C. stands for District of Columbia. Washington, D.C., has an area of 68 sq miles (176 sq km) and a population of 563,384.

Delaware

Area: 2,489 sq miles (6,447 sq km)
Population: 817,491
Capital: Dover (pop 32,808)
Largest city: Wilmington (pop 72,051)

New Jersey

Area: 8,721 sq miles (22,587 sq km)
Population: 8,638,396
Capital: Trenton (pop 85,314)
Largest city: Newark (pop 277,911)

CANADA

MAINE

Caribou
Presque Isle
Mt. Katahdin △ 5,266 feet
Chesuncook Lake
Millinocket
Moosehead Lake
Eastport
Bangor
Bucksport
Waterville
★ Augusta
Mount Desert Island

Massena
Plattsburgh
Newport
Berlin
Ogdensburg
Burlington
Lake Champlain
Montpelier
VERMONT
Mt. Marcy △ 5,345 feet
Adirondack Mts
Mt. Washington 6,290 feet
White Mts
NEW HAMPSHIRE
Auburn
Lewiston
Westbrook
Portland
Biddeford
Rutland
Claremont
Rochester
Dover
Watertown
Glens Falls
Springfield
Concord ★
Portsmouth
Utica
Bennington
Brattleboro
Nashua
Lawrence
Manchester
Lowell
Cambridge
Rochester
Auburn **Syracuse**
Finger Lakes
NEW YORK
Mohawk
Troy
Albany
Pittsfield MASSACHUSETTS
★ **Boston**
Brockton
Lake Ontario
Ithaca
Catskill Mts
Springfield
Worcester
Cape Cod
Binghamton
Hudson
Providence ★
Kingston
Hartford ★
Fall River
New Bedford
RHODE ISLAND
Poughkeepsie
CONNECTICUT
Newport
Nantucket I.
Waterbury
Martha's Vineyard
Scranton
New Haven
Susquehanna
Bridgeport
Williamsport
Stamford
Wilkes-Barre
Long Island
State College
Paterson
Newark
New York City
Sunbury
Bethlehem
Jersey City
ATLANTIC OCEAN
PENNSYLVANIA
Allentown
Elizabeth
Altoona
Harrisburg ★
Reading
NEW JERSEY
Delaware
★ **Trenton**
Norristown
Levittown
Lancaster
Philadelphia
Camden
Chambersburg
York
Wilmington
Hagerstown
Newark
Atlantic City
Frederick
Baltimore
Vineland
Winchester
MARYLAND
Dover ★
Cape May
Washington D.C. ★
Annapolis
Milford
Arlington
DELAWARE
Alexandria
Harrisonburg
Salisbury
Fredericksburg
Lexington Park
Charlottesville
VIRGINIA
Chesapeake Bay
James
Richmond ★
Potomac
Shenandoah
Petersburg
Newport News
Hampton
Portsmouth
Norfolk
Virginia Beach
MOUNTAINS

miles 0 — 100
kilometers 0 — 100

U.S. Southeastern States

 Texas

Area: 268,581 sq miles
(695,625 sq km)
Population: 22,118,509
Capital: Austin (pop 672,011)
Largest city: Houston
(pop 2,009,690)

 Oklahoma

Area: 69,989 sq miles
(181,036 sq km)
Population: 3,511,532
Capital and largest city:
Oklahoma City (pop 523,303)

 Arkansas

Area: 53,179 sq miles
(137,734 sq km)
Population: 2,725,714
Capital and largest city:
Little Rock (pop 184,053)

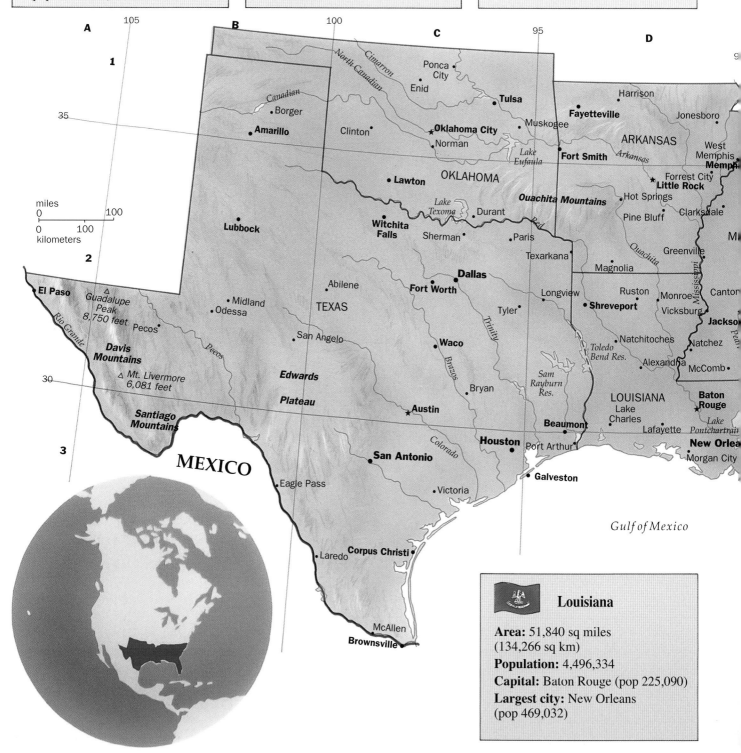

Louisiana

Area: 51,840 sq miles
(134,266 sq km)
Population: 4,496,334
Capital: Baton Rouge (pop 225,090)
Largest city: New Orleans
(pop 469,032)

Tennessee

Area: 42,143 sq miles
(109,150 sq km)
Population: 5,841,748
Capital: Nashville (pop 544,765)
Largest city: Memphis
(pop 645,978)

 North Carolina

Area: 53,819 sq miles
(139,391 sq km)
Population: 8,407,248
Capital: Raleigh (pop 316,802)
Largest city: Charlotte
(pop 584,658)

 South Carolina

Area: 32,020 sq miles
(82,932 sq km)
Population: 4,147,152
Capital and largest city:
Columbia (pop 117,357)

 Alabama

Area: 52,419 sq miles
(135,765 sq km)
Population: 4,500,752
Capital: Montgomery
(pop 200,123)
Largest city: Birmingham
(pop 236,620)

 Georgia

Area: 59,425 sq miles
(153,911 sq km)
Population: 8,684,715
Capital and largest city:
Atlanta (pop 423,019)

 Florida

Area: 65,755 sq miles
(170,305 sq km)
Population: 17,019,068
Capital: Tallahassee (pop 153,938)
Largest city: Jacksonville
(pop 773,781)

Mississippi

Area: 48,430 sq miles
(125,434 sq km)
Population: 2,881,281
Capital and largest city:
Jackson (pop 179,599)

U.S. Midwestern States

 North Dakota

Area: 70,700 sq miles
(183,113 sq km)
Population: 633,837
Capital: Bismarck (pop 56,344)
Largest city: Fargo (pop 91,484)

 South Dakota

Area: 77,116 sq miles
(199,730 sq km)
Population: 764,309
Capital: Pierre (pop 13,939)
Largest city: Sioux Falls
(pop 133,834)

 Minnesota

Area: 86,939 sq miles
(225,172 sq km)
Population: 5,059,375
Capital: St. Paul (pop 280,404)
Largest city: Minneapolis (pop
373,188)

 Nebraska

Area: 77,354 sq miles
(200,347 sq km)
Population: 1,739,291
Capital: Lincoln (pop 235,594)
Largest city: Omaha (pop 404,267)

 Kansas

Area: 82,277 sq miles
(213,096 sq km)
Population: 2,723,507
Capital: Topeka (pop 122,008)
Largest city: Wichita (pop
354,617)

Iowa

Area: 56,272 sq miles
(145,744 sq km)
Population: 2,944,062
Capital and largest city:
Des Moines (pop 196,093)

Missouri

Area: 69,704 sq miles
(180,533 sq km)
Population: 5,704,484
Capital: Jefferson City (pop 37,550)
Largest city: Kansas City
(pop 442,768)

Wisconsin

Area: 65,498 sq miles
(169,640 sq km)
Population: 5,472,299
Capital: Madison (pop 218,432)
Largest city: Milwaukee (pop
586,941)

Michigan

Area: 96,716 sq miles
(250,494 sq km)
Population: 10,079,985
Capital: Lansing (pop 118,379)
Largest city: Detroit (pop
911,402)

Ohio

Area: 44,825 sq miles
(116,097 sq km)
Population: 11,435,798
Capital and largest city:
Columbus (pop 728,432)

Indiana

Area: 36,418 sq miles
(94,323 sq km)
Population: 6,195,643
Capital and largest city:
Indianapolis (pop 783,438)

Illinois

Area: 57,914 sq miles
(149,997 sq km)
Population: 12,653,544
Capital: Springfield (pop 113,586)
Largest city: Chicago (pop
2,869,121)

U.S. Western States

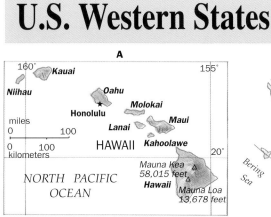

A

160° **Kauai**
Niihau
Oahu **Molokai**
Honolulu ★ **Maui**
Lanai
Kahoolawe
HAWAII
155°

miles
0   100
0   100
kilometers
20°

NORTH PACIFIC
OCEAN

Mauna Kea
58,015 feet △
Hawaii
Mauna Loa △
13,678 feet

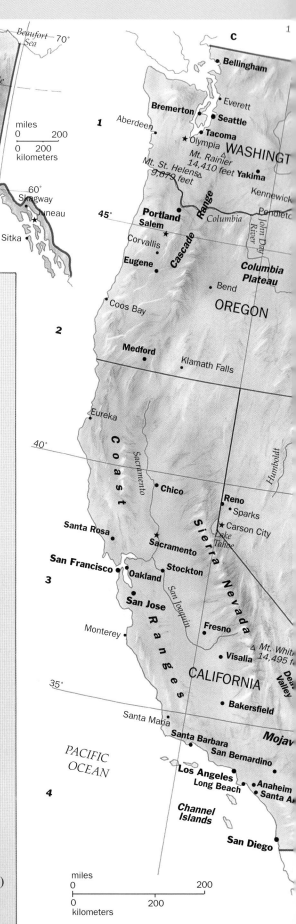

Barrow B Beaufort —70°
Bering Strait Sea
Brooks Range
Nome ALASKA
Arctic Circle
Yukon
Fairbanks
Alaska △ Range
Mt. McKinley
20,323 feet
● Anchorage
miles
0   200
0   200
kilometers
60°
Seward Skagway
Bering Gulf of Juneau ★
Sea Kodiak Alaska
Island Sitka
Aleutian Islands NORTH PACIFIC
160° OCEAN 140°

C 1
● Bellingham
Bremerton ● Everett
Aberdeen ● Seattle
★ Olympia ● Tacoma WASHINGT
Mt. Rainier Yakima
14,410 feet
Mt. St. Helens △
9,679 feet Kennewick
Range Columbia Pendlet
45° Portland John Day
Salem ★ Columbia River
Corvallis Cascade
Eugene Columbia
Plateau
● Bend
● Coos Bay OREGON
Medford
● Klamath Falls
Eureka
Coast Sacramento Humboldt
40° Chico
Reno
● Sparks
Santa Rosa ★ Carson City
Sacramento Lake
San Francisco ● Tahoe
Oakland ● Stockton
San Joaquin
San Jose
Monterey ● Fresno
Ranges ● Mt. Whit
Visalia 14,495 f
35° CALIFORNIA Death
● Bakersfield Valley
Santa Maria
Santa Barbara Mojav
San Bernardino
PACIFIC Los Angeles ● Anaheim
OCEAN Long Beach Santa A
Channel
Islands
San Diego

Hawaii

Area: 10,931 sq miles
(28,311 sq km)
Population: 1,257,608
Capital and largest city: Honolulu
(pop 380,149)

Alaska

Area: 663,267 sq miles
(1,717,862 sq km)
Population: 648,818
Capital: Juneau (pop 31,187)
Largest city: Anchorage (pop
270,951)

Washington

Area: 71,300 sq miles
(184,667 sq km)
Population: 6,131,445
Capital: Olympia (pop 43,963)
Largest city: Seattle (pop 569,101)

Idaho

Area: 83,570 sq miles
(216,446 sq km)
Population: 1,366,332
Capital and largest city: Boise
(pop 190,117)

Oregon

Area: 98,381 sq miles
(254,807 sq km)
Population: 3,559,596
Capital: Salem (pop 142,914)
Largest city: Portland (pop
538,544)

Nevada

Area: 110,561 sq miles
(286,352 sq km)
Population: 2,241,154
Capital: Carson City (pop 55,311)
Largest city: Las Vegas
(pop 517,017)

California

Area: 163,696 sq miles
(423,973 sq km)
Population: 35,484,453
(California has a larger population
than any other state in the United
States)
Capital: Sacramento (pop 445,335)
Largest city: Los Angeles (pop
3,819,951)

miles
0   200
0   200
kilometers

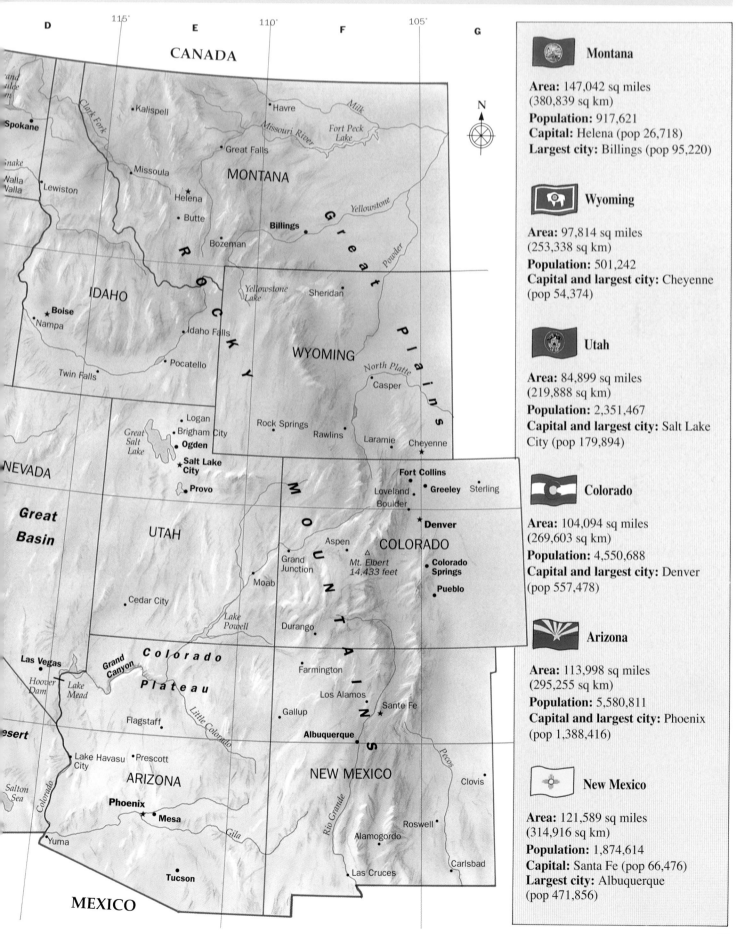

Montana

Area: 147,042 sq miles
(380,839 sq km)
Population: 917,621
Capital: Helena (pop 26,718)
Largest city: Billings (pop 95,220)

Wyoming

Area: 97,814 sq miles
(253,338 sq km)
Population: 501,242
Capital and largest city: Cheyenne
(pop 54,374)

Utah

Area: 84,899 sq miles
(219,888 sq km)
Population: 2,351,467
Capital and largest city: Salt Lake
City (pop 179,894)

Colorado

Area: 104,094 sq miles
(269,603 sq km)
Population: 4,550,688
Capital and largest city: Denver
(pop 557,478)

Arizona

Area: 113,998 sq miles
(295,255 sq km)
Population: 5,580,811
Capital and largest city: Phoenix
(pop 1,388,416)

New Mexico

Area: 121,589 sq miles
(314,916 sq km)
Population: 1,874,614
Capital: Santa Fe (pop 66,476)
Largest city: Albuquerque
(pop 471,856)

Mexico and Central America

MEXICO

Area: 761,606 sq miles (1,972,556 sq km)

Highest point: Citlaltépetl (also called Orizaba) 18,555 ft (5,656 m)

Population: 104,959,594

Capital and largest city: Mexico City (pop 8,605,239; pop of metropolitan area 18,660,000)

Other cities:
Guadalajara (3,697,000)
Monterrey (3,267,000)
Puebla (1,888,000)

Official language: Spanish

Religion: Christianity (95%)

Main products: Oil, silver, machinery and other manufactures, farm products

Currency: Mexican Peso

Government: Federal republic (official name: United Mexican States)

BELIZE

Area: 8,867 sq miles (22,966 sq km)

Population: 272,945

Capital: Belmopan (pop 9,000)

Largest city: Belize City (pop 59,400)

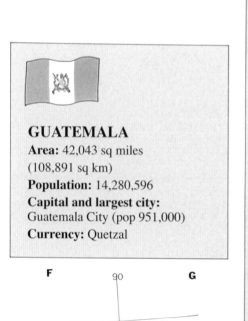

GUATEMALA
Area: 42,043 sq miles
(108,891 sq km)
Population: 14,280,596
Capital and largest city:
Guatemala City (pop 951,000)
Currency: Quetzal

EL SALVADOR
Area: 8,124 sq miles
(21,041 sq km)
Population: 6,587,541
Capital and largest city: San
Salvador (pop 1,424,000)
Official language: Spanish
Currency: Colón, U.S. Dollar

HONDURAS
Area: 42,278 sq miles
(109,500 sq km)
Population: 6,,823,568
Capital and largest city:
Tegucigalpa (pop 1,007,000)
Currency: Lempira

NICARAGUA
Area: 49,998 sq miles
(129,495 sq km)
Population: 5,359,759
Capital and largest city: Managua
(pop 1,098,000)
Official language: Spanish
Currency: Córdoba

COSTA RICA
Area: 19,730 sq miles
(51,101 sq km)
Population: 3,956,507
Capital and largest city: San José
(pop 1,085,000)
Official language: Spanish
Currency: Colón

PANAMA
Area: 30,193 sq miles
(78,200 sq km)
Population: 3,000,463
Capital and largest city:
Panama City (pop 930,000)
Official language: Spanish
Currency: Balboa

Gulf of Mexico

Tropic of Cancer

F 90 G

Mérida

Campeche Yucatán Peninsula

Campeche Bay

85 H

Villahermosa Belize City Gulf of Honduras

Coatzacoalcos Belmopan Caribbean Sea

Tuxtla Gutiérrez BELIZE

GUATEMALA San Pedro Sula

Quezaltenango HONDURAS

Tapachula Tegucigalpa

Guatemala City San Salvador

Santa Ana San Miguel NICARAGUA

EL SALVADOR León

5 Managua Lake Nicaragua

Granada

80 I

COSTA RICA Colón

miles
0   200

0   200
kilometers

10 San José Panama Canal Panama City

David PANAMA

6 Gulf of Panama

31

Caribbean

CUBA
Area: 42,803 sq miles
(110,860 sq km)
Population: 11,308,764
Capital: Havana (pop 2,189,000)

JAMAICA
Area: 4,244 sq miles
(10,992 sq km)
Population: 2,713,130
Capital: Kingston (pop 575,000)

BAHAMAS
Area: 5,382 sq miles
(13,939 sq km)
Population: 299,697
Capital: Nassau (pop 222,000)

PUERTO RICO
Area: 3,515 sq miles (9,104 sq km)
Population: 3,897,960
Capital: San Juan (pop 433,412)

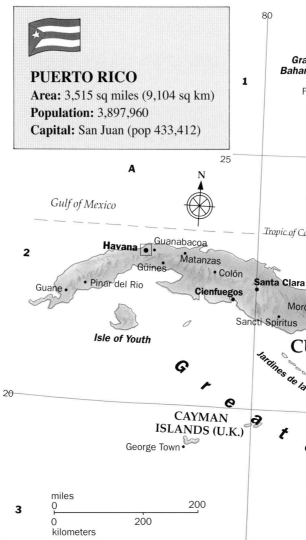

miles
0 — 200
0 — 200
kilometers

DOMINICAN REPUBLIC
Area: 18,815 sq miles
(48,731 sq km)
Population: 8,833,634
Capital and largest city: Santo
Domingo (pop 1,865,000)
Official language: Spanish
Religion: Christianity
Main products: Sugar, gold, silver,
coffee, cocoa
Currency: Peso

Caribbean Sea

HAITI
Area: 10,714 sq miles
(27,749 sq km)
Population: 7,656,166
Capital and largest city: Port-au-
Prince (pop 1,961,000)
Official languages: French and Creole
Religion: Christianity
Currency: Gourde

ANTIGUA AND BARBUDA
Area: 171 sq miles (443 sq km)
Population: 68,320
Capital: Saint John's (pop 28,000)

DOMINICA
Area: 291 sq miles (754 sq km)
Population: 69,278
Capital: Roseau (pop 27,000)

ST. KITTS and NEVIS
Area: 101 sq miles (262 sq km)
Population: 38,836
Capital: Basseterre (pop 13,000)

ST. LUCIA
Area: 238 sq miles (616 sq km)
Population: 164,213
Capital: Castries (pop 14,000)

ST. VINCENT & THE GRENADINES
Area: 150 sq miles (389 sq km)
Population: 117,193
Capital: Kingstown (pop 29,000)

FRENCH CARIBBEAN TERRITORIES:
Guadeloupe, Martinique

NETHERLANDS TERRITORIES:
Aruba, Netherlands Antilles

BRITISH TERRITORIES:
Anguilla, Cayman Islands, Montserrat, Turks and Caicos Islands, Virgin Islands

U.S. TERRITORIES:
Virgin Islands

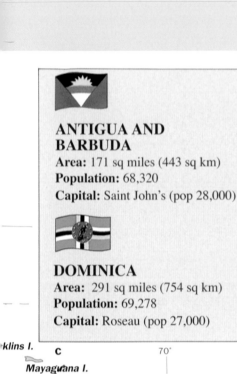

klins I.
Mayaguana I.
C
70°
TURKS & CAICOS ISLANDS (U.K.)
Great
agua I.
Grand Turk
Matthew Town

D
65°
ATLANTIC OCEAN
E
F
Cap-Haïtien
Puerto Plata
Gonaïves
Santiago
La Vega
DOMINICAN
St. Marc
REPUBLIC
Port-au-Prince
Azua
La Romana
HAITI
Santo Domingo
es Cayes Jacmel
Barahona
i l l e s

VIRGIN ISLANDS
(U.S.) (U.K.)
ANGUILLA (U.K.)
60°
Arecibo
San Juan
Road Town
Mayaguez
Ponce
Charlotte Amalie
St. Martin
ANTIGUA AND BARBUDA
PUERTO RICO (U.S.)
Basseterre
St. John's
ST. KITTS and NEVIS
MONTSERRAT (U.K.)
Plymouth
GUADELOUPE (Fr.)
L e s s e r
Basse Terre
Roseau
DOMINICA
15°
MARTINIQUE (Fr.)
Fort-de-France
A n t i l l e s
Castries
ST. LUCIA
Kingstown
BARBADOS
Bridgetown
4
ST. VINCENT & THE GRENADINES
St. George's
GRENADA
Tobago
Scarborough
TRINIDAD AND TOBAGO
Port of Spain
Trinidad
10°

GRENADA
Area: 133 sq miles (344 sq km)
Population: 89,357
Capital: St. George's (pop 33,000)

NETHERLANDS ANTILLES
ARUBA
Bonaire
Curaçao
Willemstad

BARBADOS
Area: 166 sq miles (430 sq km)
Population: 267,000
Capital: Bridgetown (pop 6,000)

TRINIDAD AND TOBAGO
Area: 1,980 sq miles (5,128 sq km)
Population: 1,096,858
Capital: Port of Spain (pop 55,000)

South America

South America is the fourth largest continent. It includes Brazil, a country which is larger than Australia. Much of the continent has a warm climate, and forests cover large areas of the north. Deserts border the coasts of west-central South America. Patagonia, in Argentina, is a dry, cold region.

The Andes Mountains, the world's longest mountain range, contain Aconcagua, South America's highest peak. The longest river is the Amazon.

South America includes 12 independent countries, French Guiana (which is ruled as part of France), and the Falkland Islands (which are ruled by Britain). South America has about 367 million people. A few people are wealthy, but the great majority are poor.

South America (Physical)

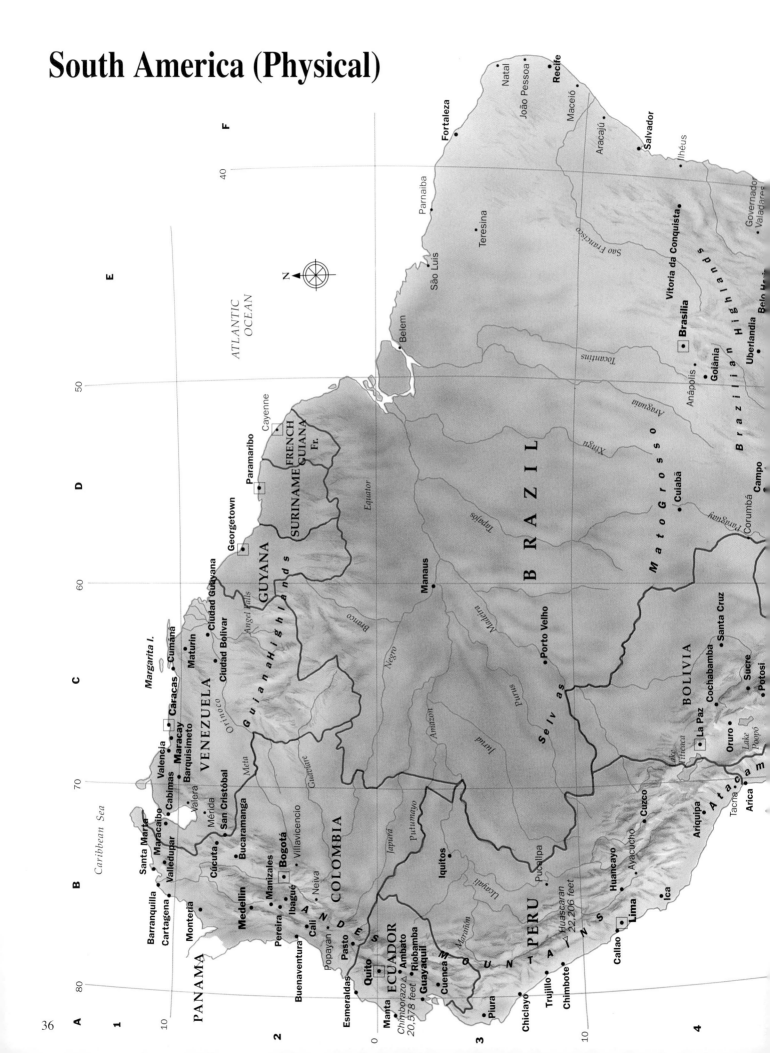

PANAMA

Caribbean Sea

Margarita I.

ATLANTIC OCEAN

N

Barranquilla
Cartagena
Santa Marta
Maracaibo
Valledupar
Cabimas
Valencia
Caracas
Cumaná
Maturín
Ciudad Bolívar
Ciudad Guayana

Montería
Valera
Mérida
San Cristóbal
Bucaramanga
Cúcuta
Villavicencio

Medellín
Manizales
Pereira
Ibagué
Bogotá
Neiva
Cali
Buenaventura
Popayán
Pasto

VENEZUELA

COLOMBIA

GUYANA
Georgetown

SURINAME
Paramaribo

FRENCH GUIANA
Fr.
Cayenne

Guiana Highlands

Orinoco
Meta
Guaviare
Angel Falls

Equator

Esmeraldas
Manta
Quito
ECUADOR
Ambato
Riobamba
Guayaquil
Cuenca
Chimborazo
20,578 feet

Chimborazo

PERU
Iquitos
Pucallpa
Piura
Chiclayo
Trujillo
Chimbote
Callao
Lima
Ica
Ayacucho
Huancayo
Cuzco
Huascarán
22,206 feet

ANDES MOUNTAINS

Japurá
Putumayo
Napo
Marañón
Ucayali

Amazon
Juruá
Purus
Madeira
Negro
Branco
Tapajós
Xingu
Tocantins
Araguaia

Manaus
Porto Velho

Selvas

BRAZIL

São Francisco

Belém
São Luís
Teresina
Parnaíba
Fortaleza
Natal
João Pessoa
Recife
Maceió
Aracajú
Salvador
Ilhéus
Vitória da Conquista
Governador Valadares

Brasília
Goiânia
Anápolis
Uberlândia
Belo Hor

Brazilian Highlands

Mato Grosso
Cuiabá
Campo
Corumbá
Paraguay

BOLIVIA
Santa Cruz
Cochabamba
Sucre
Potosí
La Paz
Oruro
Lake Titicaca
Lake Poopó

Atacama
Tacna
Arica
Arequipa

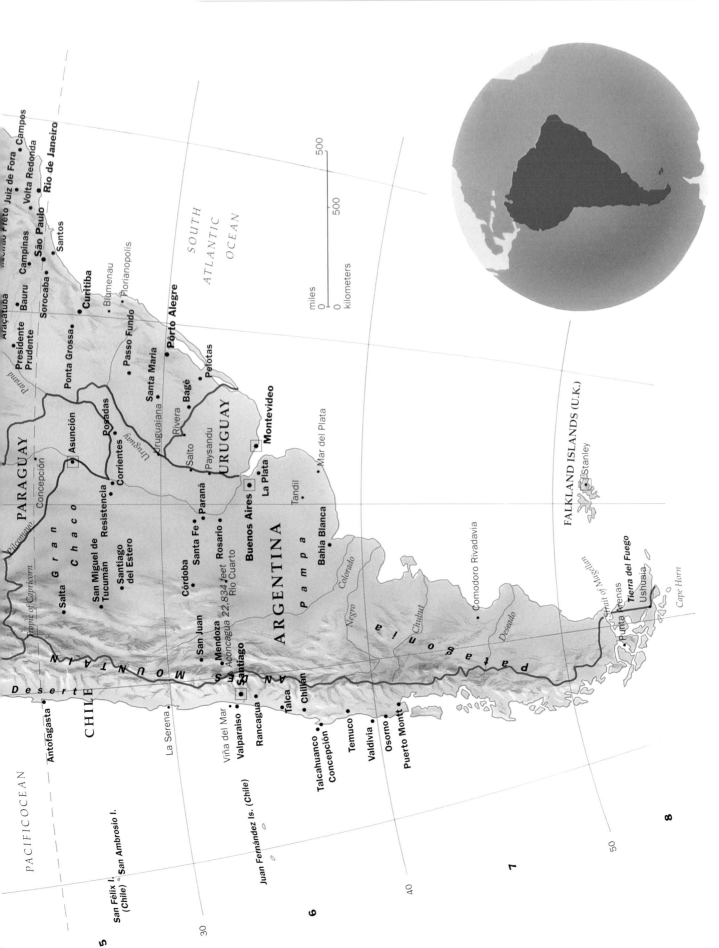

South America (Political)

COLOMBIA
Area: 493,735 sq miles
(1,138,914 sq km)
Population: 42,310,775
Capital and largest city: Bogotá
(pop 7,290,000)
Currency: Colombian Peso

VENEZUELA
Area: 352,144 sq miles
(912,053 sq km)
Population: 25,017,387
Capital and largest city: Caracas
(pop 3,226,000)
Currency: Bolivar

ECUADOR
Area: 109,483 sq miles
(283,561 sq km)
Population: 13,212,742
Capital: Quito (pop 1,451,000)
Currency: U.S. Dollar

PERU
Area: 496,226 sq miles
(1,285,225 sq km)
Population: 27,544,305
Capital and largest city: Lima
(pop 7,899,000)
Currency: Sol

BOLIVIA
Area: 424,164 sq miles
(1,098,585 sq km)
Population: 8,724,156
Capital and largest city: La Paz
(pop 1,477,000)
Currency: Boliviano

CHILE
Area: 292,260 sq miles
(756,953 sq km)
Population: 15,823,957
Capital and largest city: Santiago
(pop 5,478,000)
Currency: Chilean Peso

PANAMA

Caracas

VENEZUELA

Bogotá

COLOMBIA

Quito

ECUADOR

PERU

Lima

La Paz

BOLIVIA

CHILE

Santiago

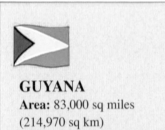

GUYANA
Area: 83,000 sq miles
(214,970 sq km)
Population: 705,803
Capital: Georgetown (pop 275,000)
Currency: Guyana Dollar

SURINAME
Area: 63,039 sq miles
(163,271 sq km)
Population: 436,935
Capital: Paramaribo (pop 253,000)
Currency: Suriname Guilder

FRENCH GUIANA (Fr.)
Area: 35,135 sq miles
(91,000 sq km)
Population: 191,309
Capital: Cayenne (pop 50,594)
Currency: Euro

BRAZIL
Area: 3,286,487 sq miles
(8,512,001 sq km)
Population: 184,101,109
Capital: Brasilia (pop 3,099,000)
Largest cities: São Paulo
(17,099,000 metropolitan area)
Rio de Janeiro (10,803,000)
Belo Horizonte (4,659,000)
Official language: Portuguese
Currency: Real

PARAGUAY
Area: 157,047 sq miles
(406,752 sq km)
Population: 6,191,368
Capital and largest city: Asunción
(pop 1,639,000)
Official languages: Spanish, Guarani
Currency: Guarani

ARGENTINA
Area: 1,068,302 sq miles
(2,766,902 sq km)
Highest point: Aconcagua 22,834 ft
(6,960 m)
Population: 39,144,753
Capital and largest city:
Buenos Aires (pop 2,776,138;
metropolitan area 13,047,000)
Official language: Spanish
Religion: Christianity
Currency: Argentine Peso

URUGUAY
Area: 68,039 sq miles
(176,221 sq km)
Population: 3,399,237
Capital and largest city:
Montevideo (pop 1,341,000)
Currency: Uruguayan Peso

FALKLAND ISLANDS (U.K.)
Area: 4,700 sq miles
(12,173 sq km)
Population: 2,967
Capital: Stanley (pop 1,989)

rgetown

Paramaribo · Cayenne

GUIANA
(Fr.)

SURINAME

YANA

BRAZIL

· Brasilia

PARAGUAY

· Asunción

URUGUAY

· Montevideo

Buenos
Aires

RGENTINA

FALKLAND ISLANDS (U.K.)

Stanley

Europe

Europe is the second smallest continent; only Australia is smaller. It contains parts of the former Soviet Union including Belarus, Moldova, Ukraine, Estonia, Latvia, Lithuania, and part of the Russian Federation, the world's largest country and one of the few countries located in more than one continent.

The highest peak in Europe is Mount Elbrus in the Caucasus Mountains, which form part of the border between Europe and Asia. The longest river, the Volga, is in the Russian Federation and flows into the Caspian Sea.

Europe also contains the world's smallest country, Vatican City, which is situated in Rome, the capital of Italy.

Europe's population of about 704 million, including the European part of Russia, is greater than that of any other continent except Asia and Africa.

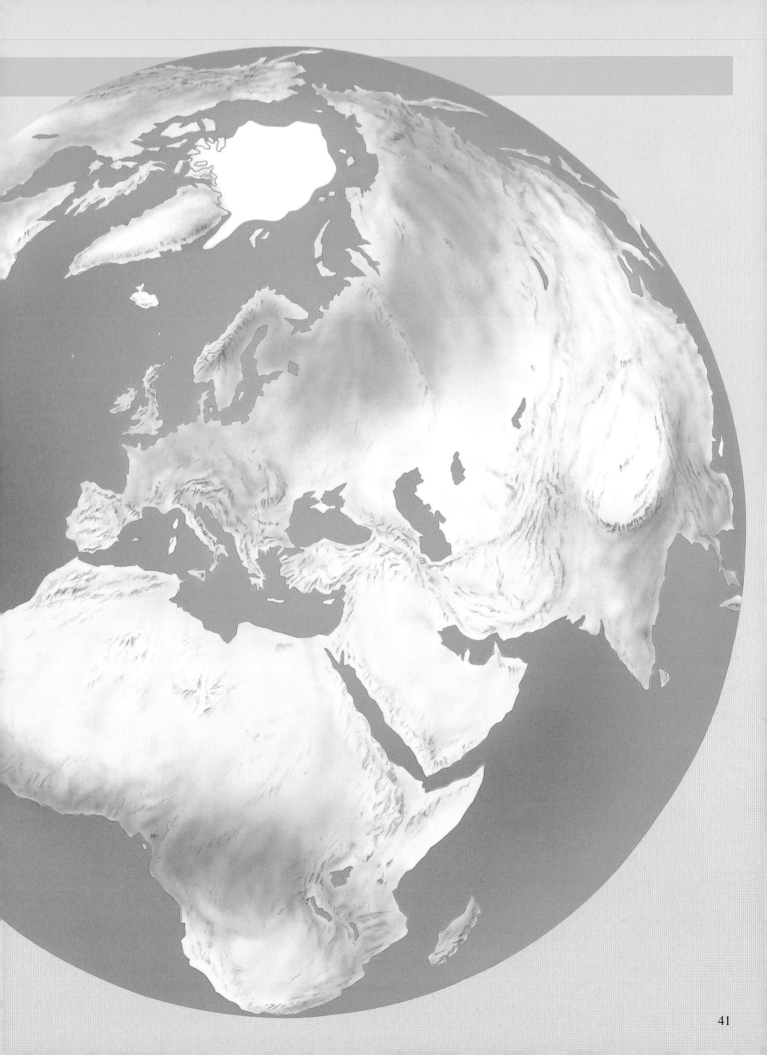

France, Belgium, and Switzerland

FRANCE

Area: 211,209 sq miles
(547,031 sq km)

Highest point:
Mont Blanc 15,771 ft (4,807 m)

Longest river:
Loire 634 miles
(1,020 km)

Population: 60,424,213

Capital and largest city:
Paris (pop 2,125,246;
metropolitan area 9,794,000)

Other cities:
Lyon (1,362,000)
Marseille (1,357,000)
Lille (1,007,000)

Official language: French

Religions: Christianity (83-88%),
Islam (5%-10%%)

Economy: *Agriculture:* beef and
dairy products, corn (maize), fruits,
grapes (for wine making), potatoes,
sugar beet, wheat; *Fishing:* sea-
fishing; *Mining:* iron ore, bauxite,
potash; *Industry:* aircraft, cars and
other transportation equipment,
chemicals, electronic equipment,
processed foods, such as cheese,
iron and steel, luxury goods, such
as perfume, machinery, textiles

Currency: Euro
Government: Republic

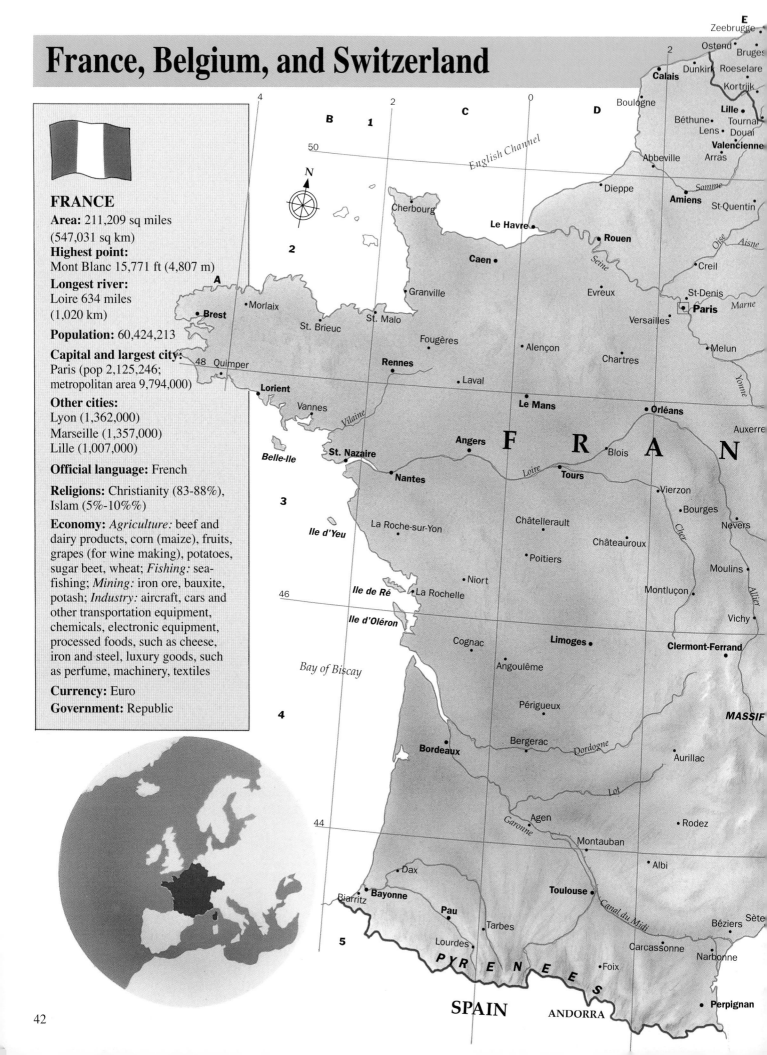

BELGIUM

Turnhout
Antwerp
Aalst · Mechelen · Genk
Hasselt
Brussels · Liège
Mons · Charleroi · Namur
Maubeuge
Verviers

Charleville-Mézières
Esch-sur-Alzette
Reims · Thionville
Épernay · Metz · Forbach
St. Dizier · Nancy
Strasbourg
Chaumont · St-Dié · Colmar
Troyes

Mulhouse
Schaffhausen · Konstanz
Belfort · Baden · Winterthur
Montbéliard · Basel · Zürich · St. Gallen
Dijon · Besançon · Olten
Solothurn · Luzern · Vaduz
La Chaux-de-Fonds · Biel
Neuchâtel · Bern · Chur
Châlon-sur-Saône · Fribourg · Thun · Davos
Lausanne · St Moritz
Mâcon · Montreux
Bourg-en-Bresse · Brig · Locarno
Roanne · Geneva · Zermatt · Lugano
Annecy
Matterhorn 14,692 feet
Lyon · Villeurbanne · Mt Blanc 15,771 feet
St-Etienne · Vienne · Chambéry
CENTRAL
Puy · Isère · Grenoble
Valence
Montélimar

Alès
Avignon
Nîmes
Montpellier · Arles
Nice · MONACO
Aix-en-Provence · Cannes
Marseille · St. Tropez
Toulon

Bastia
Mt. Cinto 8,892 feet
CORSICA
Ajaccio

MEDITERRANEAN SEA

Gulf of Lion

LUXEMBOURG
Luxembourg

FRANCE
E

GERMANY

Lake Constance

LIECHTENSTEIN

SWITZERLAND

AUSTRIA

ITALY

ALPS

JURA Mts
Lake Neuchâtel
Lake Geneva

VOSGES Mts
Rhine
Meuse
Saône
Rhône
Isère
Durance

MONACO

miles
0   50

0   50
kilometers

BELGIUM

Area: 11,786 sq miles (30,526 sq km)

Population: 10,348,276
Capital: Brussels (pop 998,000)
Official languages: Dutch, French, German

Economy: Chemicals, coal, dairy products, meat, steel, textiles
Currency: Euro
Government: Parlimentary democracy/constitutional monarchy

LUXEMBOURG

Area: 998 sq miles (2,585 sq km)

Population: 462,690

Capital: Luxembourg (pop 77,000)

Principal languages: French, German, Luxembourgish

Economy: banking, iron and steel, food processing, chemicals

Government: Constitutional monarchy

SWITZERLAND

Area: 15,942 sq miles (41,290 sq km)

Population: 7,450,867

Capital: Bern (pop 320,000)
Official languages: German, French, Italian

Economy: Manufacturing, including watches and precision instruments; agriculture, especially dairy products; tourism; banking

Currency: Swiss Franc
Government: Federal republic

MONACO

Area: <1 sq mile (1.95 sq km)

Population: 32,270

Capital: Monaco (pop 1,100)

Government: Constitutional monarchy

LIECHTENSTEIN

Area: 62 sq miles (158 sq km)

Population: 33,436

Capital: Vaduz (pop 4,900)

Government: Hereditary constitutional monarchy

British Isles

UNITED KINGDOM

Area: 94,525 sq miles
(244,820 sq km)
Highest point: Ben Nevis,
Scotland, 4,406 ft (1,343 m)
Population: 60,270,708
Capital and largest city: London
(pop 7,619,000)
Other cities:
Birmingham (2,243,000)
Manchester (2,223,000)
Leeds (1,417,000)
Glasgow (1,168,270)
Liverpool (924,000)
Official language: English
Religions: Christianity (72%),
Islam (3%), many others
Economy: *Agriculture:* wheat,
barley, potatoes, sugar beet,
livestock, dairy products; *Fishing:*
wet fish, shellfish; *Mining:* coal,
oil and natural gas, tin, iron ore;
Industry: machinery and
transportation equipment, metals,
food processing, paper
Currency: Pound Sterling
Government: Constitutional
monarchy, whose official name
is the United Kingdom of Great
Britain and Northern Ireland
(or U.K.). Great Britain consists
of England, Scotland, and Wales.

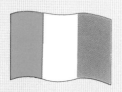

IRELAND

Area: 27,135 sq miles
(70,280 sq km)
Highest point: Carrauntoohil
3,414 feet (1,041 m)
Population: 3,969,558
Capital and largest city: Dublin
(pop 495,781)
Official languages: Irish, English
Religions: Christian (95%),
Main products: brewing, textiles,
clothing, pharmaceutical chemicals
Currency: Euro
Government: Parlimentary republic

Countries in the U.K.
England
Area: 50,333 sq miles
(130,362 sq km)
Population: 49,138,831
Capital: London (pop 7,619,000)

Northern Ireland
Area: 5,452 sq miles
(14,121 sq km)
Population: 1,702,600
Capital: Belfast (pop 277,000)

Scotland
Area: 30,418 sq miles
(78,783 sq km)
Population: 5,057,400
Capital: Edinburgh (pop 449,000)

Wales
Area: 8,019 sq miles
(20,769 sq km)
Population: 2,938,200
Capital: Cardiff (pop 305,000)

D 4

Thurso • John o'Groats

• Wick

6 ornoway Lochinver

North West Highlands

E 2 **F**

Moray Firth

Dingwall • Buckie • Fraserburgh

Skye Nairn Elgin • Peterhead

Hebrides Inverness

anna Kyle of Lochalsh *Loch Ness* *Spey*

Mallaig *Dee* • **Aberdeen**

Rhum

Muck **Eigg** △

ll Fort William *Ben Nevis*
4,406 feet • Montrose

ee **Mull** *Tay*
na • Oban Perth • **Dundee**

Colonsay **SCOTLAND** Kirkcaldy • St. Andrews

Loch Lomond Dunfermline *Firth of Forth*

Jura Dumbarton Falkirk • **Edinburgh**

Greenock **Glasgow**

Islay Paisley Motherwell Berwick-upon-Tweed

Hamilton *Clyde* *Tweed* **Holy I.**

Arran Kilmarnock Peebles Kelso **Farne Is.**

Ayr *Southern Uplands* Hawick

nt's Moffat Blyth

useway Gretna Green **Newcastle**
upon Tyne South Shields

Coleraine Dumfries *Tyne* Gateshead • **Sunderland**

NORTHERN Stranraer Carlisle Consett

IRELAND Durham • Hartlepool

Antrim • Larne Kirkcudbright *P* Stockton **Middlesbrough**

Newtownabbey *e* Workington **Lake** Penrith Darlington

gh **Belfast** *n* Whitehaven **District**

gh Lisburn *n*

Lurgan *i* △ *Scafell Pike* **North York**

tadown **Isle of** *n* 3,209 feet **Moors** Scarborough

Newry **Man** *e* Barrow-in-Furness

Mourne *s* Morecambe • Lancaster *Ouse* • Bridlington

Mts • Douglas Harrogate

• Dundalk **York**

• Drogheda *Irish Sea* Blackpool • Preston **Bradford Leeds** *Humber* **Kingston upon Hull**

Halifax Wakefield Scunthorpe

Southport **Huddersfield** • Grimsby

• Dublin Holyhead Llandudno Wigan **Manchester** Barnsley • Doncaster

Dun Laoghaire **Liverpool** **Sheffield** • Rotherham

Anglesey Bangor **Birkenhead** **Stockport** Chesterfield Lincoln

Wicklow Caernarfon Chester Crewe Mansfield Skegness

icklow *Snowdon* Wrexham **Stoke-** **Nottingham** Boston *The*
Mts 3,560 feet **on-Trent** *Wash*

Stafford **Derby** *Trent* Grantham • King's Lynn

Wexford **WALES** Shrewsbury Burton **Leicester** *The Fens* • Great Yarmouth

Aberystwyth *Cambrian Mts* **Walsall** **ENGLAND** **Peterborough** **Norwich**
Wolverhampton *Great Ouse* • Lowestoft

Birmingham • **Coventry**

Llandrindod Wells Worcester Northampton • Cambridge

Fishguard Hereford Banbury Bedford **Ipswich**

St. George's Channel Cheltenham Colchester

Carmarthen Merthyr **Luton**

Milford Haven Tenby Llanelli Neath Tydfil Gloucester **Oxford** St. Albans • Clacton-on-Sea

Pembroke Aberdare *Cotswolds* **Chilterns** Chelmsford

Swansea **Newport** Swindon **London** **Southend-on-Sea**

Port **Bristol** *Severn* Chatham • Margate

Talbot Bath **Reading** *Thames*

Cardiff Weston-super-Mare Basingstoke **North Downs** Canterbury

Guildford • Dover

Lundy I. Barnstaple Bridgwater Salisbury Winchester Tunbridge Ashford Folkestone

Exmoor Taunton **South Downs** Wells • Hastings

• Yeovil **Southampton**

Exeter **Portsmouth** **Brighton** Eastbourne

Bodmin **Bournemouth** *Strait of Dover*

Moor **Dartmoor** **Torquay** Weymouth **Isle of Wight**

St. Austell *English Channel*

Truro **Plymouth**

Penzance

Land's End

Isles of Scilly

G | **Orkney Islands**
59 • Kirkwall
Thurso
• Wick
3

H | **Shetland Islands**
Lerwick
60
2 *Fair Isle* 1

North Sea

H
Channel Islands
Alderney
Guernsey
St. Peter Port **Sark**
Jersey
St. Helier
FRANCE
49
3

45

Spain and Portugal

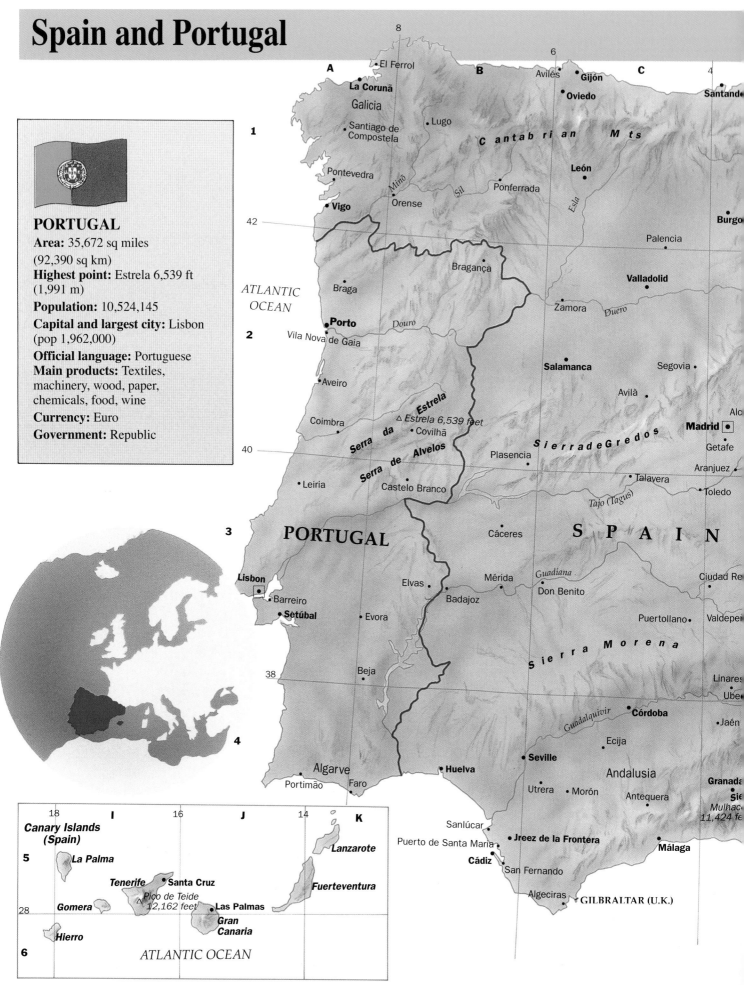

PORTUGAL

Area: 35,672 sq miles (92,390 sq km)

Highest point: Estrela 6,539 ft (1,991 m)

Population: 10,524,145

Capital and largest city: Lisbon (pop 1,962,000)

Official language: Portuguese

Main products: Textiles, machinery, wood, paper, chemicals, food, wine

Currency: Euro

Government: Republic

ATLANTIC OCEAN

A

El Ferrol
La Coruña
Galicia
Santiago de Compostela
Pontevedra
Vigo
Orense
Lugo
Miño
Sil

1

B

Avilés
Gijón
Oviedo
C a n t a b r i a n   M t s
León
Ponferrada
Esla

C

Santand...

42

Braga
Bragança
Burgo...
Palencia
Valladolid
Zamora
Duero
Salamanca
Segovia
Avilà
Madrid
Getafe
Aranjuez
Alc...

Porto
Vila Nova de Gaia
Douro
2

Aveiro

Estrela
△ Estrela 6,539 feet
Covilhã
Serra da
Serra de Alvelos
S i e r r a d e G r e d o s

40

Coimbra

Leiria
Castelo Branco
Plasencia
Talavera
Tajo (Tagus)
Toledo

3

PORTUGAL
Cáceres
Mérida
Guadiana
Don Benito
S P A I N
Ciudad Re...
Puertollano
Valdepe...

Lisbon
Barreiro
Setúbal
Evora
Elvas
Badajoz

38
Beja

S i e r r a   M o r e n a
Linares
Ube...

4

Algarve
Portimão
Faro

Huelva

Guadalquivir
Córdoba
Jaén
Ecija
Seville
Andalusia
Granad...
Utrera
Morón
Antequera
Sie...
Mulhac...
11,424 fe...

Sanlúcar
Puerto de Santa Maria
Jreez de la Frontera
Málaga
Cádiz
San Fernando
Algeciras
GILBRALTAR (U.K.)

---

18   I   16   J   14   K

Canary Islands (Spain)

5
La Palma
Lanzarote

Tenerife Santa Cruz
Fuerteventura

28
Gomera
△ Pico de Teide 12,162 feet
Las Palmas
Hierro
Gran Canaria

6
ATLANTIC OCEAN

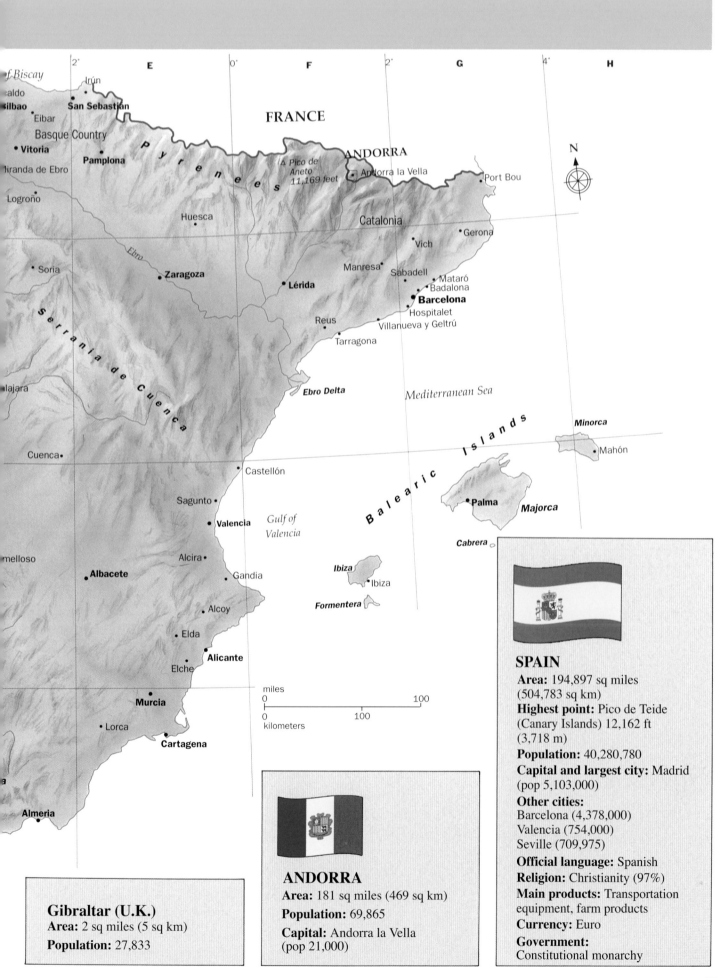

f Biscay

Irún

aldo
ilbao
San Sebastián

Eibar

Basque Country

Vitoria

Pamplona

liranda de Ebro

Logroño

FRANCE

P y r e n e e s

△ Pico de
Aneto
11,169 feet

ANDORRA

Andorra la Vella

Port Bou

N

Huesca

Catalonia

Gerona

Vich

Soria

Ebro

Zaragoza

Manresa

Sabadell

Lérida

Mataró
Badalona

Barcelona

Hospitalet

Reus

Villanueva y Geltrú

Tarragona

S e r r a n i a   d e   C u e n c a

lajara

Ebro Delta

Mediterranean Sea

Minorca

Mahón

Cuenca

B a l e a r i c   I s l a n d s

Castellón

Sagunto

Palma

Majorca

Valencia

*Gulf of
Valencia*

Cabrera

Alcira

melloso

Ibiza

Albacete

Gandia

Ibiza

Alcoy

Formentera

Elda

Alicante

Elche

miles
0   100

0   100
kilometers

Murcia

Lorca

Cartagena

Almeria

SPAIN
Area: 194,897 sq miles
(504,783 sq km)
Highest point: Pico de Teide
(Canary Islands) 12,162 ft
(3,718 m)
Population: 40,280,780
Capital and largest city: Madrid
(pop 5,103,000)
Other cities:
Barcelona (4,378,000)
Valencia (754,000)
Seville (709,975)
Official language: Spanish
Religion: Christianity (97%)
Main products: Transportation
equipment, farm products
Currency: Euro
Government:
Constitutional monarchy

ANDORRA
Area: 181 sq miles (469 sq km)
Population: 69,865
Capital: Andorra la Vella
(pop 21,000)

Gibraltar (U.K.)
Area: 2 sq miles (5 sq km)
Population: 27,833

Northwestern Europe

Arctic Circle

24° **A** 20° **B** 16° **C**

1

Ísafjördhur • 66°

• Siglufjördhur

• Akureyri

ICELAND

• Seydhisfjördhur

2

Vatnajökull (Glacier)

Reykjavik • □

Keflavik • • Hafnarfjördhur

• Hofn

△ Hvannadalshnúkur 6,952 feet

Heimaey I. ▢

◊ *Surtsey I.*

Faroe Is. (Denmark)

62° • Tórshavn

7°

3

D 8° **E** 70° 12° **F** 16° **1** **G** 20° **H**

Hammerfes

Norwegian Sea

• Alta

• Tromso

Lofoten Islands

• Harstad

L a p l a

• Narvik

Kebnekaise △ 6,966 feet

• Bodø

Arctic Circle

66°

• Kiruna

• Gällivare

• Boden

Ke

• Skellefte

• Luleå

62°

• Ålesund

• Molde

• Namsos

• Steinkjer

Trondheim

• Skellefteå

Ume

• Östersund

• Örnsköldsvik

• Umeå

Gulf of Bothnia

• Kokkola

NORWAY

ATLANTIC OCEAN

Jostedal Glacier

△ Glittertind 8,104 feet

Ljungan

• Härnösand

• Sundsvall

• Vaasa

Sogne Fiord

4

Bergen •

Haugesund •

Hardanger Plateau

• Lillehammer

Glåma

• Gjøvik • Hamar

• Ringerike

SWEDEN

• Falun

• Borlänge

• Gävle

• Sandviken

• Pori

Tampere

• Rauma

• Hämeenlinna

Stavanger •

• Drammen

□ **Oslo**

Klar

Åland Islands

Turku •

Vanta

58°

• Kristiansand

• Skien

• Moss

Fredrikstad

• Karlstad

• Örebro

Lake Vänern

Västerås

Uppsala

• Eskilstuna

□ **Stockholm**

Espoo

Hels

• Arendal

North Sea

Skagerrak

• Frederikshaven

Lake Vättern

• Uddevalla

Norrköping

Linköping

Baltic Sea

5

Borås

Göteborg

Jönköping

• Visby

Gotland

Holstebro •

Jutland

Ålborg

• Randers

Kattegat

• Halmstad

• Växjö

Herning •

Århus

DENMARK

Esbjerg •

• Kolding

Odense

• Slagelse

Copenhagen

□

Helsingborg

• Lund

Malmö

• Kalmar

• Kristianstad

Öland

• Karlskrona

GERMANY

Bornholm

miles
0 ——— 100

0 ——— 100
kilometers

48

Vadso

Lake
Inari

N

Kemi

niemi Kemijärvi

RUSSIA

Kajaani

NLAND

Lake
Pielinen

Kuopio

Lake
Callavesi

Joensuu

Lake
Orives

äskylä

Lake
Kokon Selka

ne

Lappeenranta

Kouvola

Kotka

f Finland

ICELAND
Area: 39,769 sq miles
(103,002 sq km)
Population: 293,966
Capital: Reykjavik (pop 184,000)
Main export: Fish and fish
products
Currency: Icelandic Króna
Government: Constitutional republic

NORWAY
Area: 125,182 sq miles
(324,221 sq km)
Population: 4,574,560
Capital: Oslo (pop 795,000)
Main export: Oil and natural gas
Currency: Norwegian Krone
Government:
Hereditary constitutional monarchy

SWEDEN
Area: 173,732 sq miles
(449,966 sq km)
Population: 8,986,400
Capital: Stockholm (pop 1,697,000)
Main exports: Machinery and
transportation equipment, wood
and wood pulp, chemicals
Currency: Swedish Krona
Government: Constitutional monarchy

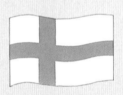

FINLAND
Area: 130,128 sq miles
(337,032 sq km)
Population: 5,215,512
Capital: Helsinki (pop 1,075,000)
Main exports: Metal products and
machinery, paper, wood and wood
products
Currency: Euro
Government: Constitutional republic

DENMARK
Area: 16,639 sq miles (43,095 sq
km) not including the Faroe
Islands and Greenland
Population: 5,413,392
Capital: Copenhagen (pop 1,066,000)
Main exports: Machinery and
instruments, food products
Currency: Danish Krone
Government: Constitutional monarchy

Germany and North-Central Europe

A 6 B 10 C 14 D

1
North Sea
Frisian Islands
Baltic Sea
Flensburg
Kiel
Neumunster
Stralsund
Slupsk
Leeuwarden
Wilhelmshaven
Bremerhaven
Lübeck
Wismar
Rostock
Koszalin
Groningen
Hamburg
Schwerin
Neustrelitz
Szczecin
Bydgoszcz
NETHERLANDS
Haarlem
Oldenburg
Bremen
Pila
Inowrocla
52
Amsterdam
Enschede
Osnabrück
Hanover
Berlin
Warta
The Hague
Utrecht
Braunschweig
Potsdam
Poznan
Rotterdam
Arnhem
Bielefeld
Saltzgitter
Magdeburg
Oder
Breda
Eindhoven
Münster
GERMANY
Halberstadt
Dessau
Cottbus
Neisse
Kalisz
Maastricht
Duisburg
Dortmund
Harz Mts
Halle
Elbe
Krefeld
Essen
Kassel
Leipzig
Görlitz
Legnica
Wroclaw
BELGIUM
Düsseldorf
Wuppertal
Erfurt
Gera
Dresden
Liberec
Sudeten Mts
Walbrzych
Opole
2
Aachen
Cologne
Chemnitz
Usti nad
Labem
Bonn
Plauen
Zwickau
Ore Mts
Hradec Králové
Ostrav
Koblenz
Giessen
Thuringian Forest
Kladno
CZECH
Eifel
Wiesbaden
Frankfurt am Main
Prague
Pardubice
Olomouc
Mosel
Mainz
Offenbach
Schweinfurt
Main
Bamberg
Plzen
Pribram
REPUBLIC
Žili
Trier
Darmstadt
Würzburg
Bohemian Forest
Jihlava
Rhine
Mannheim
Heidelburg
Nuremburg
Saarbrücken
Heilbronn
Regensburg
Êeské
Budêjovice
Brno
Vah
Karlsruhe
FRANCE
Black Forest
Stuttgart
Danube
Znojmo
Freiburg
Ulm
Augsburg
Inn
Krems
Linz
Vienna
Bratislava
48
Ravensburg
Munich
Wels
Steyr
St. Pölten
3
SWITZERLAND
Lake Constance
Dornbirn
Salzburg
Enns
Wiener Neustadt
Lake Neusiedler
Györ
Innsbruck
Alps
AUSTRIA
Leoben
Szombathely
ITALY
△ Gross Glockner
12,461 feet
Graz
Mur
Székesfehérvar
Villach
Klagenfurt
Lake Balaton
Drava
Nagykanizsa
SLOVENIA
Péc
CROATIA
Go

NETHERLANDS

Area: 16,033 sq miles
(41,525 sq km)

Population: 16,318,199

Capital: Amsterdam (pop 1,145,000)

Official language: Dutch

Main exports: Machinery and
transportataion equipment, food,
chemicals, mineral fuels, metals

Currency: Euro

Government: Parlimentay
democracy under constitutional
monarch

E N 22 F

RUSSIA LITHUANIA

•Elblag

Olsztyn

•Lomza
Bialystok

Wloclawek

•ck *Vistula* Bug

Warsaw ▪ •Siedlce BELARUS

POLAND

•Łódź

•Piotrków Pulawy
Radom •Lublin

•Czestochowa •Kielce

Zamość

ze
orzów *Vistula* San
owice Jaroslaw
Kraków Rzeszów•
Przemysl

Carpathian Mts

△ Gerlachovka Stit
8,711 feet

SLOVAK REPUBLIC UKRAINE

Košice

•Miskolc

Debrecen

Budapest *Tisza*

UNGARY

ecskémét Békéscsaba

Hódmezővásárhely ROMANIA

Szeged•

ERBIA &
ONTENEGRO

miles
0   100

0   100
kilometers

GERMANY
Area: 137,847 sq miles
(357,024 sq km)
Population: 82,424,609
Capital: Berlin (pop 3,327,000)
Other cities:
Hamburg (2,670,000)
Munich, or München (2,300,000)
Cologne, or Köln (963,200)
Frankfurt am Main (644,700)
Official language: German
Religions: Christianity (68%),
Islam (4%)
Economy: *Agriculture:* barley
wheat, rye, potatoes, sugar beet;
Fishing: cod, herring; *Mining:* coal,
lignite, iron, potash; *Industry:*
machinery and transportation
equipment, motor vehicles,
chemicals and chemical products
Currency: Euro
Government: Federal republic

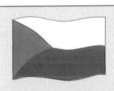

CZECH REPUBLIC
Area: 30,450 sq miles
(78,866 sq km)
Population: 10,246,178
Capital: Prague (pop 1,170,000)
Currency: Czech Koruna

SLOVAK REPUBLIC
Area: 18,859 sq miles
(48,845 sq km)
Population: 5,423,567
Capital: Bratislava (pop 425,000)
Currency: Slovak Koruna

POLAND
Area: 120,728 sq miles
(312,686 sq km)
Population: 38,626,349
Capital: Warsaw (pop 2,200,000)
Main exports: Machinery and
transportation equipment
Currency: Zloty
Government: Republic

AUSTRIA
Area: 32,382 sq miles
(83,869 sq km)
Population: 8,174,762
Capital: Vienna (pop 2,179,000)
Main exports: Machinery and
transportation equipment
Currency: Euro
Government: Federal republic

HUNGARY
Area: 35,919 sq miles
(93,030 sq km)
Population: 10,032,375
Capital: Budapest (pop 1,708,000)
Main exports: Machinery
Currency: Forint
Government:
Parlimentary democracy

Italy and Southeastern Europe

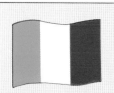

ITALY

Area: 116,306 sq miles
(301,233 sq km)
Population: 58,057,477
Capital: Rome (pop 2,665,000)
Other large cities:
Milan (4,183,000)
Naples (2,995,000)
Turin (1,247,000)
Official language: Italian
Religion: Christianity (90%)
Currency: Euro

VATICAN CITY (in Rome)

Area: 109 acres (44 hectares)
Population: 921

SAN MARINO

Area: 24 sq miles (62 sq km)
Population: 28,503
Capital: San Marino (pop 5,000)

SLOVENIA

Area: 7,827 sq miles (20,272 sq km)
Population: 2,011,473
Capital: Ljubljana (pop 256,000)

SERBIA & MONTENEGRO

Area: 39,518 sq miles
(102,352 sq km)
Population: 10,825,900
Capital: Belgrade (pop 1,118,000)

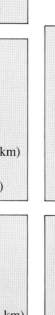

CROATIA

Area: 21,831 sq miles (56,542 sq km)
Population: 4,496,869
Capital: Zagreb (pop 688,000)

BOSNIA & HERZEGOVINA

Area: 19,741 sq miles (51,129 sq km)
Population: 4,007,608
Capital: Sarajevo (pop 579,000)

MALTA

Area: 122 sq miles (316 sq km)
Population: 396,851
Capital: Valletta (pop 83,000)

SWITZERLAND
AUSTRIA
Bolzano
Dolomites
Maribor
Mt. Rosa 15,204 feet
Mont Blanc 15,775 feet
Lake Maggiore
Lake Como
Trento
Udine
SLOVENIA
Zagreb
Matterhorn 14,689 feet
Como
Bergamo
Lake Garda
Treviso
Ljubljana
FRANCE
Novara
Milan
Vicenza
Trieste
Rijeka
CROATIA
Turin
Brescia
Verona
Padua
Venice
Pavia
Ticino
Adda
Cremona
Adige
Po
Ferrara
Pula
Prijed
Alessandria
Piacenza
Parma
Modena
Una
Banja L
Genoa
Reggio nell'Emilia
Bologna
Ravenna
BOSN
La Spezia
Apennine
Forlì
Rimini
Zadar
Lucca
Prato
San Marino
Pisa
Florence
SAN MARINO
Split
Leghorn
Arno
Ancona
Ligurian Sea
Arezzo
Perugia
Adriatic Sea
Siena
Elba
ITALY
Ascoli Piceno
Corsica
Terni
Mt. Corno △ 9,561 feet
Tiber
L'Aquila
Pescara
Rome
M ts
Foggia
Sassari
Olbia
miles
0   100
Barletta
Ba
Sardinia
0   100
kilometers
Naples
Vesuvius △ 4,190 feet
Potenza
Ischia
Salerno
Taranto
Oristano
Arbatax
Capri
Tyrrhenian Sea
Cagliari
Cosenza
Catanzaro
Ustica
Lipari Is.
Trapani
Palermo
Messina
Reggio di Calabria
Mt. Etna △ 10,959 feet
Enna
Catania
Caltanissetta
Pantelleria
Sicily
Siracusa
Ragusa
Mediterranean S
MALTA
Valletta

Map labels

N

D E UKRAINE 26

HUNGARY

Satu Mare
Baia Mare
Oradea
Cluj-Napoca
Botosani
Iasi
Piatra Neamt
Bacau

MOLDOVA
F

Somesul

Subotica
Arad
Alba Iulia
Mures
Tigu Mures
ROMANIA
Sibiu
Brasov
Buzau
Braila
Galati
Siret
Mouths of Danube

Timisoara

ijek
Novi Sad
Resita
Transylvanian Alps
Tirgu-Jiu
Pitesti
Ploesti
Bucharest
Constanta

vonski Brod
Belgrade
Drobeta-Turnu Severin
Olt
Danube
Craiova
Ruse
Razgrad
Silistra
Tolbukhin

Tuzla
Smederevo
Valjevo
Kragujevac
GOVINA
Cacak
Kraljevo
Morava
ajevo
Drina
SERBIA & MONTENEGRO
Nis
Pleven
Shumen
Varna
Black Sea

ar
Novi Pazar
Leskovac
Balkan Mts
BULGARIA
Sliven
Burgas

nik Podgorica
Pec
Urosevac
Pernik
Sofia
Stara Zagora
Yambol

Lake Scutari
Pristina
Plovdiv
Khaskovo

Shkodër
Skopje
Titov Veles
Rhodope Mts
Strima

Goshvar
Vardar
MACEDONIA
Komotini

Tirana
Elbasan
Bitola
Kavalla
Maritsa

Durrës
Serrai
Thasos

ALBANIA
Veroia
Thessaloniki
Samothráki

disi
Korce
TURKEY

Vlore
Mt. Olympus 9,571 feet
Mt. Athos 6,670 feet
Limnos

ecce
Pinios
Larisa
Aegean Sea
Lésvos

Corfu
Pindus Mts
Ioannina
Volos
Skiros
Khios

Ionian Sea
Levkás
Agrinion
GREECE
Lamia
Khalkis
Euboea
Khios

Kefallinia
Patras
Athens
Piraeus
Andros
Tinos
Ikaria
Samos

Zákinthos
Argos
Kithnos
Naxos
Kos

Kalamata
Milos
Thira
Rhodes
Rhodes

Kithira
Karpathos

Khania
Iraklion

Crete

Country information boxes

ROMANIA
Area: 91,699 sq miles (237,500 sq km)
Population: 22,355,551
Capital: Bucharest (pop 1,853,000)
Currency: Leu

BULGARIA
Area: 42,823 sq miles (110,912 sq km)
Population: 7,517,973
Capital: Sofia (pop 1,076,000)
Currency: Lev

ALBANIA
Area: 11,100 sq miles (28,749 sq km)
Population: 3,544,808
Capital: Tirana (pop 367,000)
Currency: Lek

GREECE
Area: 50,942 sq miles (131,940 sq km)
Population: 10,647,529,000
Capital: Athens (pop 3,215,000)
Official language: Greek
Currency: Euro

MACEDONIA
Area: 9,781 sq miles (25,333 sq km)
Population: 2,071,210
Capital: Skopje (pop 447,000)

Russia and Its Neighbors

RUSSIAN FEDERATION (RUSSIA)

Area: 6,592,769 sq miles (17,075,271 sq km), the world's largest country

Highest point: Mount Elbrus 18,510 ft (5,642 m)

Population: 143,782,338

Capital: Moscow (pop 10,469,000)

Other cities:
St. Petersburg (5,214,000)
Novosibirsk (1,426,000)
Nizhniy Novgorod (1,331,000)
Yekaterinburg (1,293,537)
Samara (1,157,880)

Official language: Russian

Religions: Christianity, Judaism, Islam

Main products: *Agriculture:* cotton, flax, potatoes, sugar, wheat, cattle, pigs, sheep; *Mining:* coal, copper, gold, iron ore, oil and natural gas; *Industry:* iron and steel, chemicals, machinery, paper, plastics

Currency: Rouble

Government: Federal republic

ESTONIA

Area: 17,462 sq miles (45,227 sq km)
Population: 1,341,664
Capital: Tallinn (pop 391,000)

LATVIA

Area: 24,938 sq miles (64,589 sq km)
Population: 2,306,306
Capital: Riga (pop 733,000)

LITHUANIA

Area: 25,174 sq miles (65,201 sq km)
Population: 3,607,899
Capital: Vilnius (pop 549,000)

BELARUS

Area: 80,155 sq miles (207,601 sq km)
Population: 10,310,520
Capital: Minsk (pop 1,705,000)

UKRAINE

Area: 233,090 sq miles (603,703 sq km)
Population: 47,732,079
Capital: Kiev (pop 2,618,000)

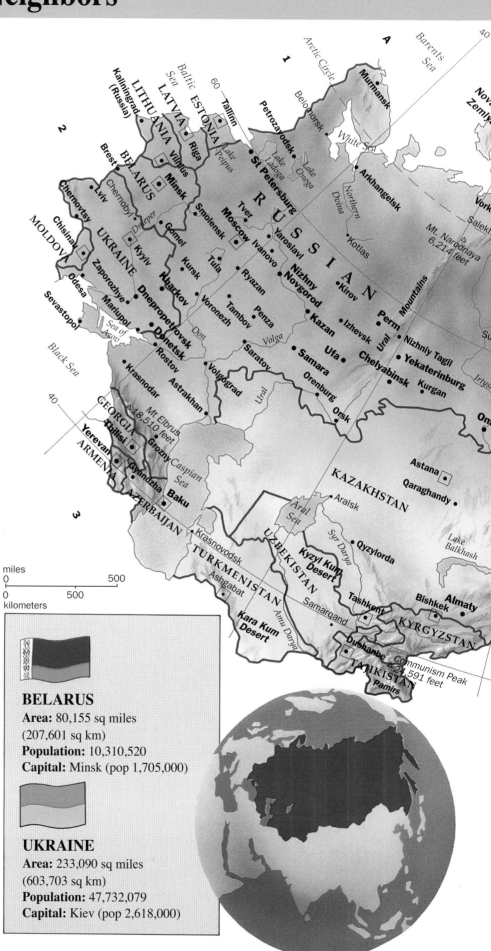

miles
0   500
0   500
kilometers

ARCTIC OCEAN

N

Severnaya Zemlya

Kara Sea

•Dikson

Nordvik

Laptev Sea

New Siberian Islands

East Siberian Sea

Wrangel I.

•Provideniya

•Anadyr

Bering Sea

Indigirka

Kolyma

Verkhoyansk Range

Kolyma Mts

Central Siberian Plateau

Lower Tunguska

Yenisey

rian Plain

Yakutsk•

Lena

Aldan

•Magadan

Kamchatka Peninsula

Δ Klyuchevskaya 15,585 feet

Okhotsk•

Sea of Okhotsk

Petropavlosk- Kamchatskiy

F E D E R A T I O N

Ob

Angara

•Tomsk

Achinsk•

osibirsk •Kemerovo

•Krasnoyarsk

•Bratsk

Nizhneudinsk•

arnaul

•Novokuznetsk

Biysk

Sayan Mts

•Cheremkhovo

Angarsk• •Chita

Irkutsk• Ulan Ude•

palatinsk

Altai Mts

Lake Baykal

Yablonovyy Range

Stanovoy Range

Amur

•Blagoveshchensk

Komsomolsk•

•Khabarovsk

Sakhalin Island

Yuzhno- •Sakhalinsk

Kuril Islands

•Vladivostok

Sea of Japan

MOLDOVA
Area: 13,067 sq miles (33,844 sq km)
Population: 4,446,455
Capital: Chisinau (pop 662,000)

GEORGIA
Area: 26,911 sq miles (69,700 sq km)
Population: 4,693,892
Capital: Tbilisi (pop 1,064,000)

ARMENIA
Area: 11,506 sq miles (29,801 sq km)
Population: 2,991,360
Capital: Yerevan (pop 1,079,000)

AZERBAIJAN
Area: 33,436 sq miles (86,599 sq km)
Population: 7,868,385
Capital: Baku (pop 1,816,000)

TURKMENISTAN
Area: 188,456 sq miles (488,101 sq km)
Population: 4,863,169
Capital: Ashgabat (pop 574,000)

KAZAKHSTAN
Area: 1,049,155 sq miles (2,717,314 sq km)
Population: 15,143,704
Capital: Astana (pop 332,000)

UZBEKISTAN
Area: 172,742 sq miles (447,402 sq km)
Population: 26,410,416
Capital: Tashkent (pop 2,155,000)

KYRGYZSTAN
Area: 76,641 sq miles (198,500 sq km)
Population: 26,410,416
Capital: Bishkek (pop 806,000)

TAJIKISTAN
Area: 55,251 sq miles (143,100 sq km)
Population: 7,011,556
Capital: Dushanbe (pop 544,000)

Asia

Asia is the largest continent. Along with China, Japan, and India, it contains the major part of the Russian Federation, along with several other countries that were formerly part of the Soviet Union. They include Armenia, Azerbaijan, and Georgia, which lie south of the Caucasus Mountains. The other countries are Kazakhstan, Kyrgyzstan, Tajikistan, Turkmenistan, and Uzbekistan. These countries lie between the Caspian Sea in the west and China in the east.

China's Chang Jiang (formerly called the Yangtze Kiang) is the longest river in Asia. Mount Everest, on Nepal's border with China, is Asia's highest peak.

Asia has almost four billion people, including the Asian part of Russia. It includes the world's two most populous countries, China and India, both with over one billion people.

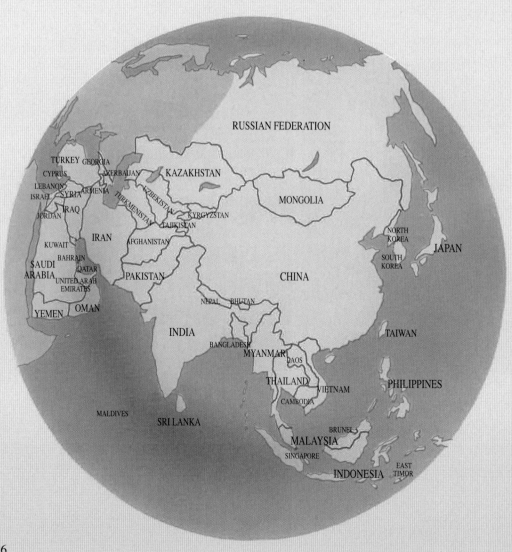

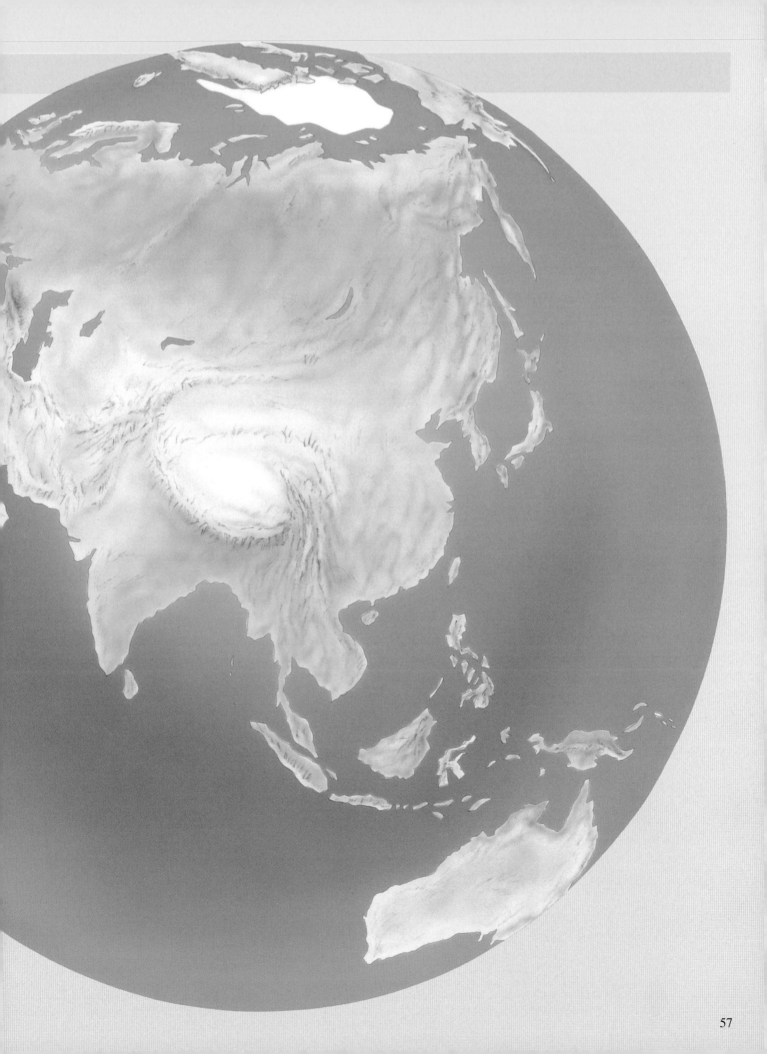

Near East

CYPRUS
Area: 3,571 sq miles (9,249 sq km)
Population: 775,927
Capital and largest city: Nicosia
(pop 205,000)

ISRAEL
Area: 8,019 sq miles
(20,769 sq km)
Population: 6,199,008
Capital: Jerusalem
(pop 686,000)
Other large cities:
Tel Aviv-Yafo (2,752,000)
Haifa (865,000)
Official languages: Hebrew, Arabic
Religions: Judaism (80%), Islam
(15%), Christianity (2%)
Currency: New Shekel

TURKEY
Area: 301,383 sq miles
(780,582 sq km)
Population: 68,893,918
Capital: Ankara (pop 3,428,000)
Other large cities:
Istanbul (8,744,000)
Izmir (2,216,000)
Bursa (1,194,687)
Adana (1,130,710)
Official language: Turkish
Religion: Islam (99.8%)
Currency: Turkish Lira

LEBANON
Area: 4,015 sq miles
(10,399 sq km)
Population: 3,777,218
Capital and largest city: Beirut
(pop 1,792,000)
Currency: Lebanese Pound

JORDAN
Area: 35,637 sq miles
(92,300 sq km)
Population: 5,611,202
Capital and largest city: Amman
(pop 1,237,000)
Currency: Jordanian Dinar

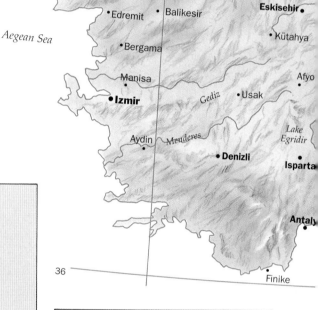

GREECE

A   28   B

1

Edirne

Tekirdag   Istanbul   Üsküdar

Sea of
Marmara   Izmit

Adapaz

Gokceada I.   Dardanelles

40   Çanakkale   Bursa

Troy

N

Edremit   Balikesir   Eskisehir

Aegean Sea   Kütahya

Bergama

Manisa   Afyo

2   Izmir   Gediz   Usak

miles   Lake
0   100   Aydin   Menderes   Egridir

0   100   Denizli   Isparta
kilometers

Antal

36   Finike

32

32

C

36

D

40

E

44

F

Zonguldak

Samsun

Black Sea

Trabzon

Rize

GEORGIA

Kars

ARMENIA

Çankiri

Corum

Kizil

Kelkit

Aras

Erzincan

Erzurum

Mt. Ararat
19,946 feet

IRAN

Ankara

Sivas

Malatya

Elazig

Lake
Van

Van

TURKEY

*Lake
Tuz*

Kayseri

Maras

Diyarbakir

Batman

Tigris

K U R D I S T A N

Nusaybin

*Lake
Beysehir*

Konya

Karaman

Seyhan

Osmaniye

Gaziantep

Urfa

Tarsus

Adana

Mersin

Ceyhan

Iskenderun

*Assad
Reservoir*

IRAQ

Silifke

Antakya

Aleppo

Euphrates

Deir-ez-Zor

Khabur

∴ Ebla

CYPRUS

Nicosia

Famagusta

Larnaca

Latakia

Hama

S Y R I A

Mari ∴

Paphos

Limassol

Krak des Chevaliers

Homs

Palmyra

Tripoli

LEBANON

Mediterranean Sea

Beirut

Zahlé

Anti-Lebanon Mts

Damascus

S y r i a n

Sidon

Tyre

D e s e r t

Golan
Heights

*Lake
Tiberias*

Haifa

Irbid

Busra

ISRAEL

Jordan

Ramat
Gan

Nablus

Zarqa

Tel Aviv-Yafo

*West
Bank*

Amman

Holon

Jerusalem

*Dead
Sea*

Hebron

JORDAN

SAUDI ARABIA

Gaza Strip

Beersheba

*Negev
Desert*

EGYPT

Petra

Ma'an

Elat

Aqaba

4

SYRIA

Area: 71,498 sq miles
(185,180 sq km)
Population: 18,016,874
Capital and largest city: Damascus
(pop 2,228,000)
Other large cities: Aleppo
(2,188,000)
Official language: Arabic
Currency: Syrian Pound

Arabian Peninsula and Gulf States

IRAQ

Area: 168,754 sq miles
(434,073 sq km)
Population: 25,374,691
Capital and largest city: Baghdad
(pop 5,620,000)
Other large cities:
Arbil (2,369,000)
Official language: Arabic
Currency: Iraqi Dinar

SAUDI ARABIA

Area: 756,985 sq miles
(1,960,582 sq km)
Population: 25,795,938
Capital: Riyadh (pop 5,126,000)
Other large cities:
Jiddah (3,171,000)
Official language: Arabic
Currency: Saudi Riyal

Map labels

A   40   B   45   C   50

N

1

TURKEY

Khvoy
Aras
Tabriz · Ardabil
Caspian Sea
Orumiyeh · Lake Urmia
Zanjan · Rasht
Elburz
Ba
Mosul · Kurdistan
Irbil ·
Qazvin · Demavend M
18,387 feet △
35
Kirkuk · As Sulaymaniyah
Tehran ·

SYRIA

Euphrates   Tigris

Bakhtaran · Hamadan
· Qom
· Arak
Borujerd ·
Kashan

I R A Q

2   Syrian Desert   Ar Ramadi · ☐ Baghdad   Khorramabad ·   Esfah·
Zagros
Karbala · Al Hilah   Dezful ·
An Najaf ·   · Shushtar
Al Amarah ·   Mountains
Ahvaz ·

JORDAN

An Nasiriyah ·   Khorramshahr ·
30   Ur ·   Basra ·   Abadan ·

Al Jawf ·

KUWAIT   Shi·

☐ Kuwait
Bushir

· Tabuk   A n N a f u d   Kuwait ·

· Hafar   Persian Gulf

3   · Hail

Buraydah   Al Qatif · Damman
Dhahran · ☐ Al
Al Wajh ·   BAHRAIN   Manan
25   Al Hufuf ·   D
H   QATA·
e
j
a   Medina   Riyadh ☐
Yanbu   z
Tropic of Cancer   ☐ Riyadh   Haradh ·

4   Red Sea   S A U D I

Jiddah · · Mecca   A R A B I A
· At Taif

20   R u b a l K h a l i

· Abha

5   Jizan ·   H a d r a m a u t

Farasan Is.

12,041 feet △ ☐ Sana's   YEMEN
15   Mukhalla ·
Al Hudaydah ·
Zabid ·

6   Mocha · · Taiz   · Shuqra
Aden

60

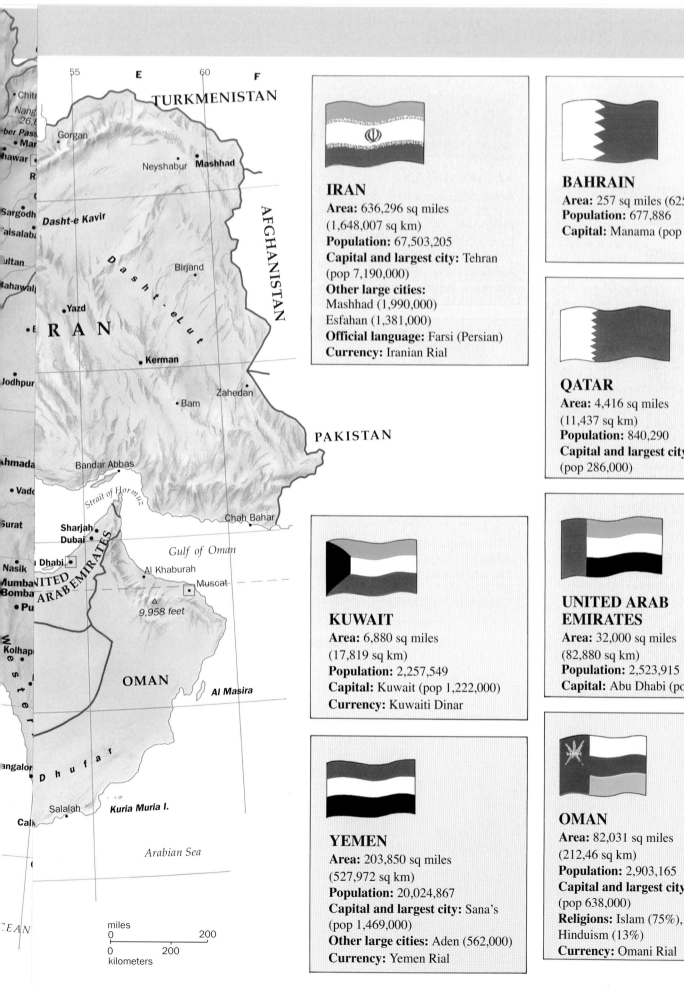

IRAN
Area: 636,296 sq miles
(1,648,007 sq km)
Population: 67,503,205
Capital and largest city: Tehran
(pop 7,190,000)
Other large cities:
Mashhad (1,990,000)
Esfahan (1,381,000)
Official language: Farsi (Persian)
Currency: Iranian Rial

BAHRAIN
Area: 257 sq miles (625 sq km)
Population: 677,886
Capital: Manama (pop 139,000)

QATAR
Area: 4,416 sq miles
(11,437 sq km)
Population: 840,290
Capital and largest city: Doha
(pop 286,000)

KUWAIT
Area: 6,880 sq miles
(17,819 sq km)
Population: 2,257,549
Capital: Kuwait (pop 1,222,000)
Currency: Kuwaiti Dinar

UNITED ARAB EMIRATES
Area: 32,000 sq miles
(82,880 sq km)
Population: 2,523,915
Capital: Abu Dhabi (pop 475,000)

YEMEN
Area: 203,850 sq miles
(527,972 sq km)
Population: 20,024,867
Capital and largest city: Sana's
(pop 1,469,000)
Other large cities: Aden (562,000)
Currency: Yemen Rial

OMAN
Area: 82,031 sq miles
(212,46 sq km)
Population: 2,903,165
Capital and largest city: Muscat
(pop 638,000)
Religions: Islam (75%),
Hinduism (13%)
Currency: Omani Rial

China, Japan, and the Far East

1 **A** 84 **B** 96 **C** 108

44

KAZAKHSTAN

Lake Uvs

Lake Hovsgol

Darhan

Erdenet

Ulaanbaatar

KYRGYZSTAN

Yining

A l t a y   M t s

MONGOLIA

TAJIKISTAN

2

Tian Shan

Urumqi

Kashi

G o b i   D e s e r t

Shache

Taklimakan Desert

PAKISTAN

A l t u n   M t s

Yumen

Baot

Kunlun Mountains

Qilian Mountains

Mu Us Desert

Yinchuan

32

Lake Qinghai

Xining

Huang He   Great Wall of Chi

Tibetan Plateau

Lanzhou

INDIA

Baoji   Xi'an

C H I N A

NEPAL

Xigaze   Lhasa

Chengdu   Nanchong

H i m a l a y a s

Everest △ 29,035 feet

Salween

Chang Jiang (Yangtze River)

3

BHUTAN

Zigong   Chongqing

Luzhou

Zunyi

Giuyang   Shaoya

Mekong

Guili

Kunming   Luizho

Yunnan Plateau   Gejiu

Xi Jiang

Wuzh

MYANMAR   VIETNAM   Nanning

LAOS

20

Zhanjiang

4

Haik

Hainan

CHINA

Area: 3,705,405 sq miles (9,596,999 sq km)

Highest point: Mount Everest, on the border with Nepal, 29,035 ft (8,848 m)

Longest river: Chang Jiang (formerly Yangtze Kiang), 3,964 miles (6,378 km)

Population: 1,298,847,624

Capital: Beijing (pop 10,848,000)

Other large cities:
Shanghai (12,887,000)
Tianjin (9,156,000)
Shenyang (4,828,000)
Wuhan (4,488,900)

Official language: Mandarin Chinese

Religions: Atheism (officially) Confucianism, Buddhism, Taoism

Economy: *Agriculture:* rice, wheat, oilseed, cotton; *Fishing*; *Mining:* coal, iron, oil; *Industry:* iron and steel, machinery, textiles

Currency: Yuan Renminbi

Government: People's republic

MONGOLIA

Area: 604,250 sq miles (1,565,008 sq km)

Population: 2,751,314

Capital and largest city: Ulaan-baatar (pop 812,000)

Principal language: Mongolian

Religions: Tibetan Buddhism Lamaism 96%

Currency: Tugrik

RUSSIA

120

D E 132 F 144

Lesser Hinggan Range

Amur

Greater Hinggan Range

•Qiqihar

•Harbin Jixi

Baicheng •Mudanjiang

Manchurian Plain

Changchun• •Jilin

Siping

Shenyang

Fuxin •Fushun

•Benxi

Jinzhou• Anshan •Hamhung

Yingkou Sinuiju

hot

Beijing Tangshan Pyongyang•

Datong •Wonsan

NORTH KOREA

•Chongjin

Sea of Japan

Tianjin• *Bo Hai Sea* Dalian Nampo •Seoul

Shijiazhuang Yantai Inchon• SOUTH KOREA

Taiyuan •Xingtai Zibo• Taejon

andan• Weifang •Qingdao Taegu

Jinan •Ulsan

Anyang *Yellow Sea* Kwangju• Pusan

Zhengzhou

•yang •Kaifeng •Lianyungang Cheju

Xuzhou

•Nanyang Huainan Nantong

•iangfan Nanjing

Hefei •Wuxi Shanghai

Wuhan Wuhu Suzhou *East China Sea*

Hangzhou•

Huangshi• •Anqing •Ningbo

•Jingdezhen

Nanchang

Changsha •Wenzhou

•Naha

•Hengyang •Fuzhou

Chilung *Ryukyu Islands*

Taipei

•Shaoguan Xiamen *Tropic of Cancer*

Taichung

Shantou Tainan TAIWAN

uangzhou Gaoxiong

•Hong Kong

Macao

South China Sea

PACIFIC OCEAN

•Asahikawa

Sapporo •Hokkaido

Hakodate

Aomori •Morioka

Akita

•Sendai

Niigata

Honshu JAPAN

•Tokyo

Kanazawa Kawasaki •Chiba

Kyoto Mt. Fuji Yokohama

Kobe Nagoya

Osaka

Sakai

Okayama

Hiroshima •Matsuyama

Kitakyushu Shikoku

Fukuoka

Nagasaki Kumamoto

Kagoshima Kyushu

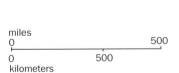

miles
0 | 500
0 | 500
kilometers

JAPAN
Area: 145,883 sq miles (377,837 sq km)
Highest point: Mount Fuji 12,388 ft (3,776 m)

Population: 127,333,002
Capital: Tokyo (pop 34,997,000)
Other large cities:
Osaka (11,165,000)
Nagoya (3,122,000)

Official language: Japanese
Religions: Shintoism and Buddhism (84%)
Main products: *Manufactures:* machinery, vehicles, electronics
Currency: Yen
Government: Parlimentary democracy

NORTH KOREA
Area: 46,541 sq miles (120,541 sq km)
Population: 22,697,553
Capital and largest city: Pyongyang (pop 3,228,000)

SOUTH KOREA
Area: 38,023 sq miles (98,480 sq km)
Population: 48,598,175
Capital and largest city: Seoul (pop 9,714,000)

TAIWAN
Area: 13,892 sq miles (35,980 sq km)
Population: 22,749,838
Capital and largest city: Taipei (pop 2,550,000)

Southeastern Asia

THAILAND
Area: 198,456 sq miles
(514,001 sq km)
Population: 64,865,523
Capital and largest city: Bangkok
(pop 6,486,000)
Principal language: Thai
Currency: Baht

MALAYSIA
Area: 127,317 sq miles
(329,751 sq km)
Population: 23,522,482
Capital and largest city: Kuala
Lumpur (pop 1,352,000)
Official language: Malay
Currency: Ringgit (Malaysian Dollar)

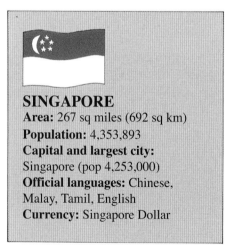

SINGAPORE
Area: 267 sq miles (692 sq km)
Population: 4,353,893
Capital and largest city:
Singapore (pop 4,253,000)
Official languages: Chinese,
Malay, Tamil, English
Currency: Singapore Dollar

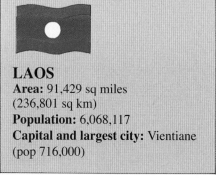

LAOS
Area: 91,429 sq miles
(236,801 sq km)
Population: 6,068,117
Capital and largest city: Vientiane
(pop 716,000)

MYANMAR (Burma)
Area: 261,970 sq km
(678,502 sq miles)
Population: 42,720,196
Capital and largest city: Yangon
(formerly Rangoon, pop 3,874,000)
Official language: Burmese
Currency: Kyat

VIETNAM
Area: 127,244 sq miles
(329,562 sq km)
Population: 82,689,518
Capital city: Hanoi (pop
3,977,000)
Currency: Dong

BRUNEI
Area: 2,228 sq miles (5,771 sq km)
Population: 365,251
Capital and largest city: Bandar
Seri Begawan (pop 61,000)

CAMBODIA
Area: 69,900 sq miles
(181,041 sq km)
Population: 13,363,421
Capital and largest city: Phnom
Penh (pop 1,157,000)
Currency: Riel

PHILIPPINES
Area: 115,831 sq miles
(300,002 sq km)
Population: 86,241,697
Capital and largest city: Manila
(pop 10,352,000)
Currency: Philippine Peso

INDONESIA
Area: 741,100 sq miles
(1,919,449 sq km)
Population: 238,452,952
Capital and largest city: Jakarta
(pop 12,296,000)
Currency: Rupiah

EAST TIMOR
Area: 5,794 sq miles
(15,006 sq km)
Population: 1,019,252
Capital: Dili (pop 49,000)

C   120°   D

Aparri

Luzon

Baguio

San Carlos

Caloocan

*South
China Sea*

■ **Manila**
Lucena

Batangas

Mindoro

△ *Mayon
Volcano
7,943 feet* **Samar**   130°   E

PHILIPPINES

Panay
Iloilo **Cadiz** *Leyte*
Bacolod **Cebu**

Negros *Bohol*

Palawan

Sulu Sea • **Butuan**
Iligan • **Cagayan de Oro**

Mindanao

Zamboanga *Mt. Apo* △ • **Davao**
Basilan *9,692 feet* • **General Santos**

*PACIFIC
OCEAN*

ar Seri Begawan   **Sabah**
BRUNEI ⌑
Tawau

Talaud Is.

Celebes Sea

Sanglhe Is.

tang **Borneo**

Manado •

Halmahera
Waigeo

140°   F

Manokwari

Sarmi

Samarinda
Palu • **Sulawesi
(Celebes)**

Obi **Misool**

New Guinea

l i m a n t a n
Balikpapan

Sula Is. *Ceram Sea*

Ceram Fakfak •

Maoke △ **Range**

*Puncak Jaya
16,503 feet*

E S I A

Banjarmasin
Majene • Kendari •

Buru • **Ambon**

**West
Papua**

**PAPUA
NEW GUINEA**

Java Sea

**Ujung
Pandang** •

Banda Sea

Aru Is.

Flores Sea

Wetar

ang
• **Surabaya**
karta
karta • **Malang** *Bali*

Lombok **Sumbawa** **Flores**

Sumba

Tanimbar Is.

Dili
Timor **EAST TIMOR**

Merauke •

67

Africa

Africa is the world's second largest continent. Much of the land is wilderness. Areas with few people include the Sahara in North Africa, the world's biggest desert, and the Kalahari and Namib Deserts in southern Africa. Africa has dense forests around the equator and huge grasslands, the home of many wild animals.

The continent's rivers include the world's longest, the Nile. The highest mountain is Kilimanjaro, an old volcano in Tanzania.

Africa contains fifty-three independent countries, with a total population of more than 870 million. A few countries are rich in minerals and some have industries, but more than half of the people of Africa are poor farmers.

North Africa

ALGERIA
Area: 919,595 sq miles
(2,381,751 sq km)
Population: 32,129,324
Capital: Algiers (pop 3,060,000)

TUNISIA
Area: 63,170 sq miles
(163,610 sq km)
Population: 9,974,722
Capital: Tunis (pop 1,996,000)

MAURITANIA
Area: 397,955 sq miles
(1,030,703 sq km)
Population: 2,998,563
Capital: Nouakchott (pop 600,000)

MOROCCO
Area: 172,414 sq miles
(446,552 sq km)
Population: 32,209,101
Capital: Rabat (pop 1,759,000)

WESTERN SAHARA
(occupied by Morocco)
Area: 102,600 sq miles
(265,734 sq km)
Population: 267,405

MALI
Area: 478,766 sq miles
(1,240,004 sq km)
Population: 11,956,788
Capital: Bamako (pop 1,264,000)

NIGER
Area: 489,191 sq miles
(1,267,005 sq km)
Population: 11,360,538
Capital: Niamey (pop 890,000)

N

ATLANTIC OCEAN

A   10°   B   0°   Algiers   C   Annaba   10°   Tunis   D

Tangier   Ceuta (Sp.)   Oran   Blida   Sétif   Constantine   Sousse
Melilla
Kenitra   Tetouan   (Sp.)   Sidi-bel-Abbès   Batna   Sfax
Rabat   Fez   Oujda   TUNISIA   Tripoli
Casablanca   Meknès   Misurata

1

Safi   Ghardaia
Marrakesh   Béchar
Agadir   Toubkal
13,665 feet
30°   MOROCCO   ALGERIA   LIBYA

Laâyoune

WESTERN
2   SAHARA
OCC. BY
MOROCCO

S   a   h   a   r   a
High Atlas Mts

Tropic of Cancer   Ahaggar Mts   Tahat
9,574 feet

Nouadhibou   Atar
20°

Air Mts

MAURITANIA   MALI   NIGER
Nouakchott   Timbuktu   S   a   h   e   l
Niger   Gao   Agades
Zinder   Lake
3   Kayes   Mopti   Maradi   Chad
Senegal   Niamey   N'Djamena
SENEGAL   Bamako   Ségou
BURKINA   NIGERIA
GUINEA   FASO   BENIN   Moundou
10°   CÔTE D'IVOIRE   CAMEROON

LIBYA
Area: 679,362 sq miles
(1,759,548 sq km)
Population: 5,6331,585
Capital: Tripoli (pop 2,006,000)

CHAD
Area: 495,755 sq miles
(1,284,005 sq km)
Population: 9,538,544
Capital: N'Djamena (pop 797,000)

EGYPT
Area: 386,662 sq miles
(1,001,455 sq km)
Population: 76,117,421
Capital: Cairo (pop 10,834,000)

ETHIOPIA
Area: 435,186 sq miles (1,127,132 sq km)
Population: 67,851,281
Capital: Addis Ababa (pop 2,723,000)

DJIBOUTI
Area: 8,880 sq miles (22,999 sq km)
Population: 466,900
Capital: Djibouti (pop 390,795)

ERITREA
Area: 46,842 sq miles (121,321 sq km)
Population: 4,447,307
Capital: Asmara (pop 556,000)

SOMALIA
Area: 246,201 sq miles
(637,661 sq km)
Population: 8,304,601
Capital: Mogadishu (pop 1,175,000)

SUDAN
Area: 967,498 sq miles
(2,505,820 sq km)
Population: 39,148,162
Capital: Khartoum (pop 4,286,000)

West Africa

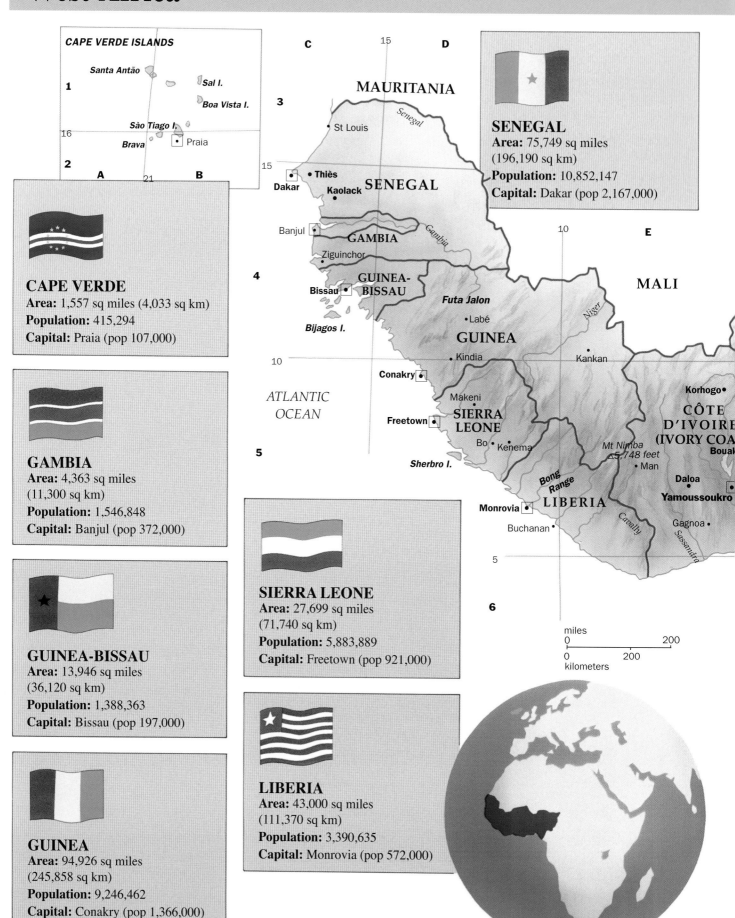

CAPE VERDE ISLANDS

Santa Antão
Sal I.
Boa Vista I.
Sào Tiago I.
Brava • Praia

1
16
2

A 21 B

C 15 D

MAURITANIA

3

St Louis

Senegal

15

• Thiès
Dakar • Kaolack SENEGAL

Banjul • GAMBIA

Gambia

Ziguinchor

4

Bissau • GUINEA-BISSAU

Futa Jalon

• Labé

Bijagos I.

GUINEA

Niger

10

ATLANTIC
OCEAN

Conakry • • Kindia

Kankan

Makeni

Freetown • SIERRA
LEONE

Bo • Kenema

5

Sherbro I.

Mt Nimba
△5,748 feet
• Man

Monrovia • LIBERIA

Buchanan •

Cavally

10

E

MALI

Korhogo •

CÔTE
D'IVOIRE
(IVORY COA

Boual

Daloa •
Yamoussoukro

Gagnoa

Sassandra

5

6

miles
0   200
0   200
kilometers

CAPE VERDE
Area: 1,557 sq miles (4,033 sq km)
Population: 415,294
Capital: Praia (pop 107,000)

GAMBIA
Area: 4,363 sq miles
(11,300 sq km)
Population: 1,546,848
Capital: Banjul (pop 372,000)

GUINEA-BISSAU
Area: 13,946 sq miles
(36,120 sq km)
Population: 1,388,363
Capital: Bissau (pop 197,000)

GUINEA
Area: 94,926 sq miles
(245,858 sq km)
Population: 9,246,462
Capital: Conakry (pop 1,366,000)

SENEGAL
Area: 75,749 sq miles
(196,190 sq km)
Population: 10,852,147
Capital: Dakar (pop 2,167,000)

SIERRA LEONE
Area: 27,699 sq miles
(71,740 sq km)
Population: 5,883,889
Capital: Freetown (pop 921,000)

LIBERIA
Area: 43,000 sq miles
(111,370 sq km)
Population: 3,390,635
Capital: Monrovia (pop 572,000)

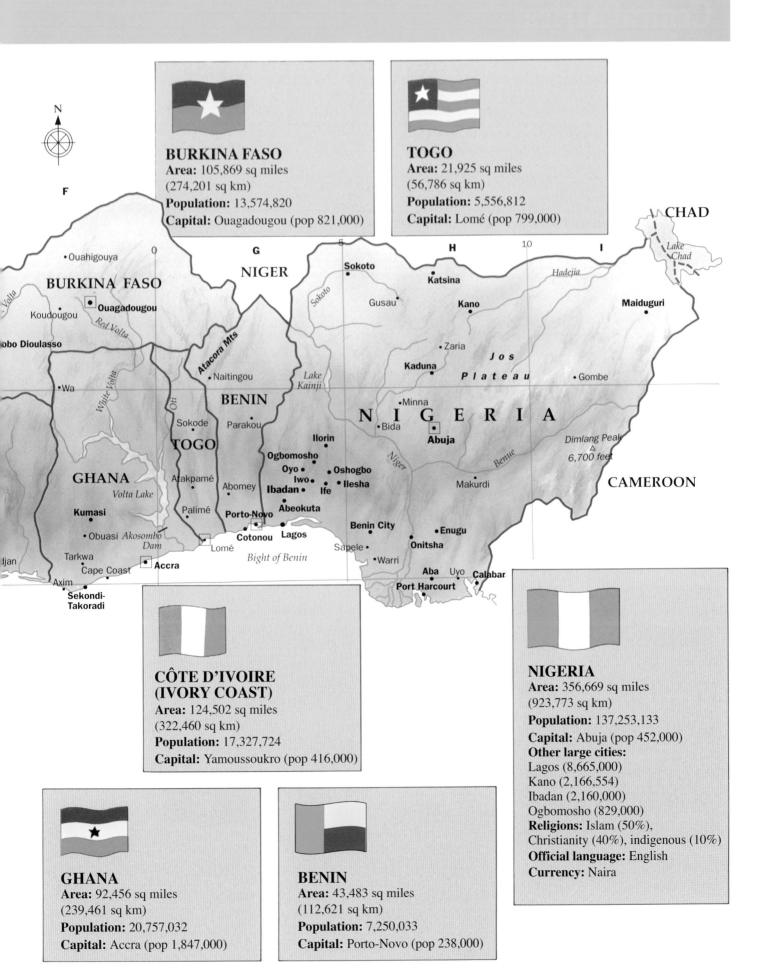

N

F

BURKINA FASO
Area: 105,869 sq miles
(274,201 sq km)
Population: 13,574,820
Capital: Ouagadougou (pop 821,000)

TOGO
Area: 21,925 sq miles
(56,786 sq km)
Population: 5,556,812
Capital: Lomé (pop 799,000)

•Ouahigouya

0

G

5

H

10

I

CHAD

Lake
Chad

BURKINA FASO

Koudougou

□ **Ouagadougou**

Red Volta

NIGER

Sokoto

• Sokoto

Hadejia

• Katsina

Gusau

• Kano

Maiduguri

obo Dioulasso

White Volta

• Wa

Ott

Atacora Mts

• Naitingou

BENIN

Lake
Kainji

• Zaria

Kaduna

J o s

P l a t e a u

• Gombe

Sokode

TOGO

Parakou

Ilorin

NIGERIA

• Minna

Dimlang Peak
6,700 feet

GHANA

Volta Lake

Atakpamé

Ogbomosho

Oyo

Abomey

Iwo

Ibadan

Oshogbo

Ilesha

Ife

• Bida

□ **Abuja**

Niger

Benue

CAMEROON

Kumasi

Palimé

Porto-Novo

Abeokuta

Makurdi

• Obuasi *Akosombo*
Dam

□

Cotonou

Lagos

Benin City

• **Enugu**

djan

Tarkwa

Lomé

Bight of Benin

Sapele •

Onitsha

Cape Coast

□ **Accra**

• Warri

• Axim

Sekondi-
Takoradi

Aba

Uyo

Calabar

Port Harcourt

CÔTE D'IVOIRE
(IVORY COAST)
Area: 124,502 sq miles
(322,460 sq km)
Population: 17,327,724
Capital: Yamoussoukro (pop 416,000)

NIGERIA
Area: 356,669 sq miles
(923,773 sq km)
Population: 137,253,133
Capital: Abuja (pop 452,000)
Other large cities:
Lagos (8,665,000)
Kano (2,166,554)
Ibadan (2,160,000)
Ogbomosho (829,000)
Religions: Islam (50%),
Christianity (40%), indigenous (10%)
Official language: English
Currency: Naira

GHANA
Area: 92,456 sq miles
(239,461 sq km)
Population: 20,757,032
Capital: Accra (pop 1,847,000)

BENIN
Area: 43,483 sq miles
(112,621 sq km)
Population: 7,250,033
Capital: Porto-Novo (pop 238,000)

Central Africa

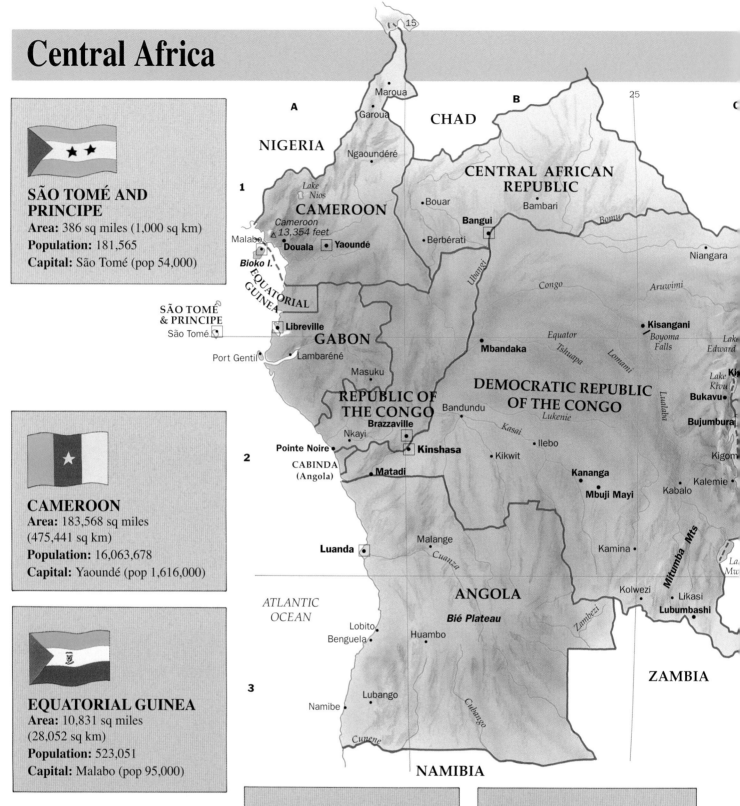

SÃO TOMÉ AND PRINCIPE
Area: 386 sq miles (1,000 sq km)
Population: 181,565
Capital: São Tomé (pop 54,000)

CAMEROON
Area: 183,568 sq miles
(475,441 sq km)
Population: 16,063,678
Capital: Yaoundé (pop 1,616,000)

EQUATORIAL GUINEA
Area: 10,831 sq miles
(28,052 sq km)
Population: 523,051
Capital: Malabo (pop 95,000)

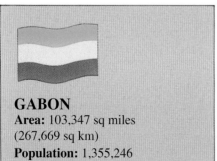

GABON
Area: 103,347 sq miles
(267,669 sq km)
Population: 1,355,246
Capital: Libreville (pop 611,000)

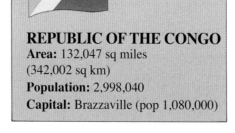

REPUBLIC OF THE CONGO
Area: 132,047 sq miles
(342,002 sq km)
Population: 2,998,040
Capital: Brazzaville (pop 1,080,000)

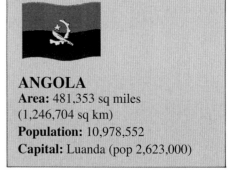

ANGOLA
Area: 481,353 sq miles
(1,246,704 sq km)
Population: 10,978,552
Capital: Luanda (pop 2,623,000)

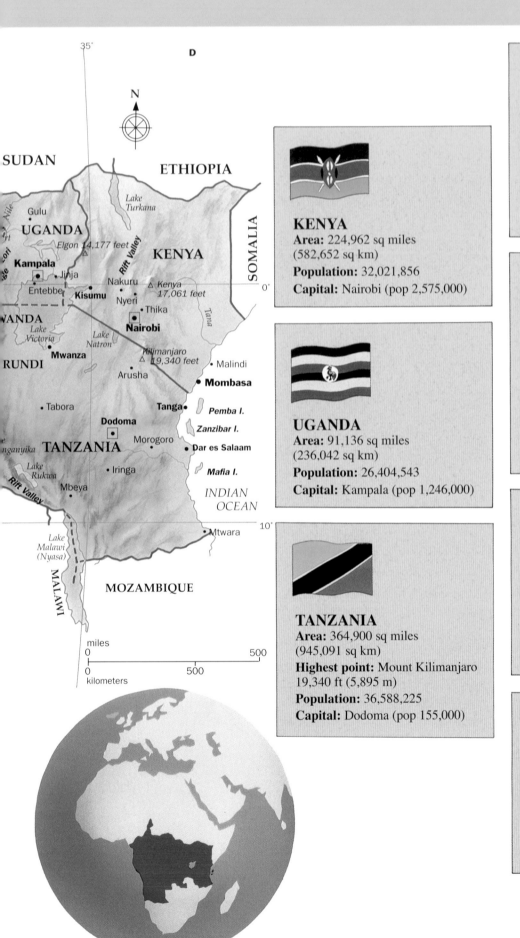

SUDAN

ETHIOPIA

N

UGANDA

Gulu

Lake Turkana

Kampala

Jinja

Entebbe

Kisumu

KENYA

SOMALIA

Elgon 14,177 feet

Nakuru

Kenya 17,061 feet

Nyeri

Thika

Nairobi

0°

RWANDA

Lake Victoria

Lake Natron

Kilimanjaro 19,340 feet

Malindi

BURUNDI

Mwanza

Arusha

Mombasa

Tabora

Tanga

Pemba I.

Dodoma

Zanzibar I.

Morogoro

Dar es Salaam

nganyika

TANZANIA

Mafia I.

Lake Rukwa

Iringa

INDIAN OCEAN

Rift Valley

Mbeya

10°

Mtwara

Lake Malawi (Nyasa)

MALAWI

MOZAMBIQUE

miles
0 — 500

0 — 500
kilometers

KENYA
Area: 224,962 sq miles
(582,652 sq km)
Population: 32,021,856
Capital: Nairobi (pop 2,575,000)

UGANDA
Area: 91,136 sq miles
(236,042 sq km)
Population: 26,404,543
Capital: Kampala (pop 1,246,000)

TANZANIA
Area: 364,900 sq miles
(945,091 sq km)
Highest point: Mount Kilimanjaro
19,340 ft (5,895 m)
Population: 36,588,225
Capital: Dodoma (pop 155,000)

CENTRAL AFRICAN REPUBLIC
Area: 240,535 sq miles
(622,986 sq km)
Population: 3,742,482
Capital: Bangui (pop 698,000)

DEMOCRATIC REPUBLIC OF THE CONGO
Area: 905,567 sq miles
(2,345,419 sq km)
Population: 58,317,930
Capital: Kinshasa (pop 5,277,000)
Official language: French
Currency: Congolese Franc

RWANDA
Area: 10,169 sq miles
(26,338 sq km)
Population: 7,954,031
Capital: Kigali (pop 656,000)

BURUNDI
Area: 10,745 sq miles
(27,830 sq km)
Population: 6,231,221
Capital: Bujumbura (pop 378,000)

Southern Africa

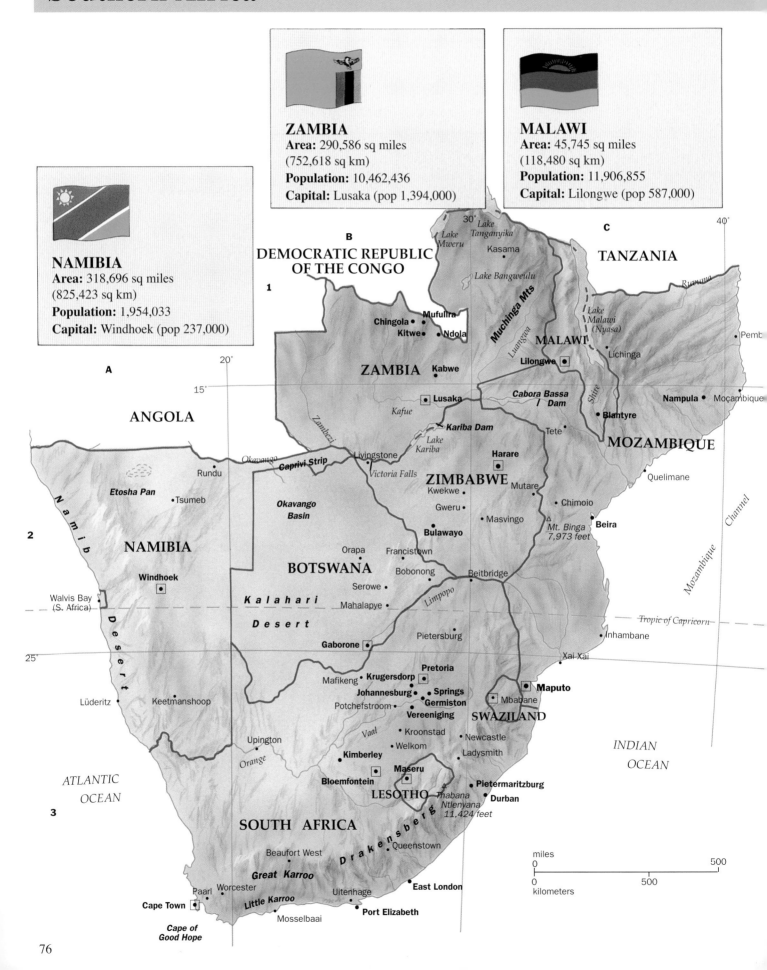

ZAMBIA
Area: 290,586 sq miles
(752,618 sq km)
Population: 10,462,436
Capital: Lusaka (pop 1,394,000)

MALAWI
Area: 45,745 sq miles
(118,480 sq km)
Population: 11,906,855
Capital: Lilongwe (pop 587,000)

NAMIBIA
Area: 318,696 sq miles
(825,423 sq km)
Population: 1,954,033
Capital: Windhoek (pop 237,000)

30°   40°

B   C

DEMOCRATIC REPUBLIC   *Lake Tanganyika*   **TANZANIA**
OF THE CONGO   *Lake Mweru*   Kasama   *Ruvuma*

1   *Lake Bangweulu*   *Lake Malawi (Nyasa)*

20°   Pemb

Mufulira   *Muchinga Mts*   Lichinga
Chingola   **MALAWI**
Kitwe • Ndola   *Luangwa*

15°   **ZAMBIA** Kabwe   *Shire*   Nampula • Moçambique

A   Lilongwe

ANGOLA   • Lusaka   *Cabora Bassa Dam*   • Blantyre

Kafue   Tete   **MOZAMBIQUE**
Zambezi   • Kariba Dam
Okavango   *Lake Kariba*   Quelimane
Livingstone
Rundu   **Caprivi Strip**   • Harare
Victoria Falls **ZIMBABWE** Mutare
Etosha Pan •Tsumeb   Kwekwe •   • Chimoio
Okavango   Gweru •
Basin   • Masvingo △ Mt. Binga Beira
                                        7,973 feet
2   **NAMIBIA**   • Bulawayo

Walvis Bay   Orapa Francistown   Beitbridge   *Mozambique Channel*
(S. Africa)   Windhoek •   **BOTSWANA** Bobonong
                          Serowe •
Namib   *Kalahari*   Mahalapye •   *Limpopo*   — *Tropic of Capricorn* —

Desert *Desert*   • Inhambane

25°   • Gaborone   Pietersburg
Lüderitz   Xai Xai

Keetmanshoop   Mafikeng • **Krugersdorp** **Pretoria**
                                      Johannesburg • **Maputo**
Upington   Potchefstroom • **Springs**   Mbabane
Orange   *Vaal*   **Vereeniging** **Germiston** **SWAZILAND**
                              • Kroonstad   **INDIAN**
                    • Welkom   • Newcastle   **OCEAN**
            Kimberley   Ladysmith
ATLANTIC   • Maseru
OCEAN   **Bloemfontein** **Pietermaritzburg**
3   **LESOTHO** *Thabana* • Durban
                              Ntlenyana
        SOUTH AFRICA *Drakensberg* 11,424 feet

                Beaufort West   Queenstown
Great Karroo
Paarl Worcester   Uitenhage **East London**
Cape Town • **Little Karroo**
                         Port Elizabeth
Cape of   Mosselbaai
Good Hope

miles
0 _____ 500
0 _____
500
kilometers

76

MOZAMBIQUE
Area: 309,496 sq miles
(801,595 sq km)
Population: 18,811,731
Capital: Maputo (pop 1,221,000)

COMOROS
Area: 838 sq miles (2,170 sq km)
Population: 651,901
Capital: Moroni (pop 53,000)

ZIMBABWE
Area: 150,804 sq miles
(390,582 sq km)
Population: 12,671,860
Capital: Harare (pop 1,469,000)

SOUTH AFRICA
Area: 471,010 sq miles
(1,219,916 sq km)
Population: 42,718,530
Capital: Pretoria (administrative,
1,209,000), Cape Town (legislative,
2,967,000), Bloemfontein (judicial,
381,000)
Other large cities:
Johannesburg (2,732,000)
Durban (2,370,000)
Religions: Christianity (68%),
indigenous beliefs and animists
(29%)
Official languages: Afrikaans,
English
Currency: Rand

BOTSWANA
Area: 231,804 sq miles
(600,372 sq km)
Population: 1,561,973
Capital: Gaborone (pop 199,000)

MADAGASCAR
Area: 226,657 sq miles
(587,042 sq km)
Population: 17,501,871
Capital: Antananarivo
(pop 1,678,000)

SWAZILAND
Area: 6,704 sq miles
(17,363 sq km)
Population: 1,169,241
Capital: Mbabane (pop 70,000)

LESOTHO
Area: 11,720 sq miles
(30,355 sq km)
Population: 1,865,040
Capital: Maseru (pop 170,000)

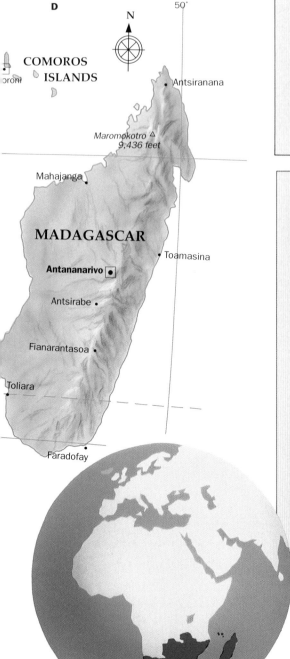

D

N

50°

COMOROS
ISLANDS

oroni

Antsiranana

Maromokotro △
9,436 feet

Mahajanga

MADAGASCAR

Antananarivo

Toamasina

Antsirabe

Fianarantsoa

Toliara

Faradofay

Australia and Oceania

Australia is the only country that is also a continent. It is the smallest of the world's seven continents. Australia is part of a region called Oceania, which also includes New Zealand, Papua New Guinea, and many islands of the Pacific Ocean.

The longest river in Australia is the Murray. It flows throughout the year, unlike the slightly longer Darling River, parts of which dry up in winter. Papua New Guinea has the highest mountains in Oceania. New Zealand's highest peak is Mount Cook. Australia's is Mount Kosciusko.

Australia is a mainly dry continent, with only about twenty million people. Most Australians live in a few cities on the coast, including Sydney and Melbourne. The rest of Oceania has about eleven million people.

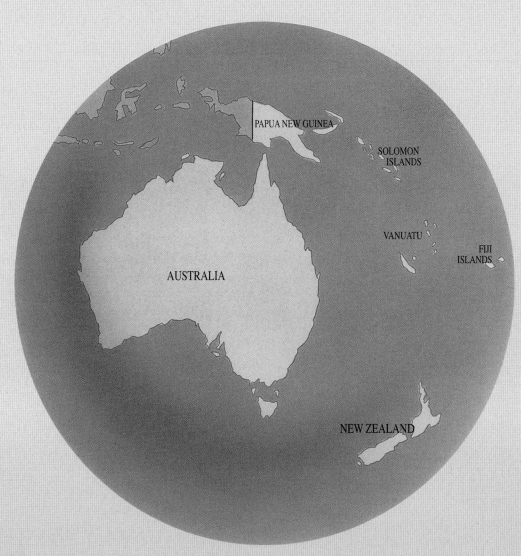

Australia, New Zealand, and the Pacific Islands

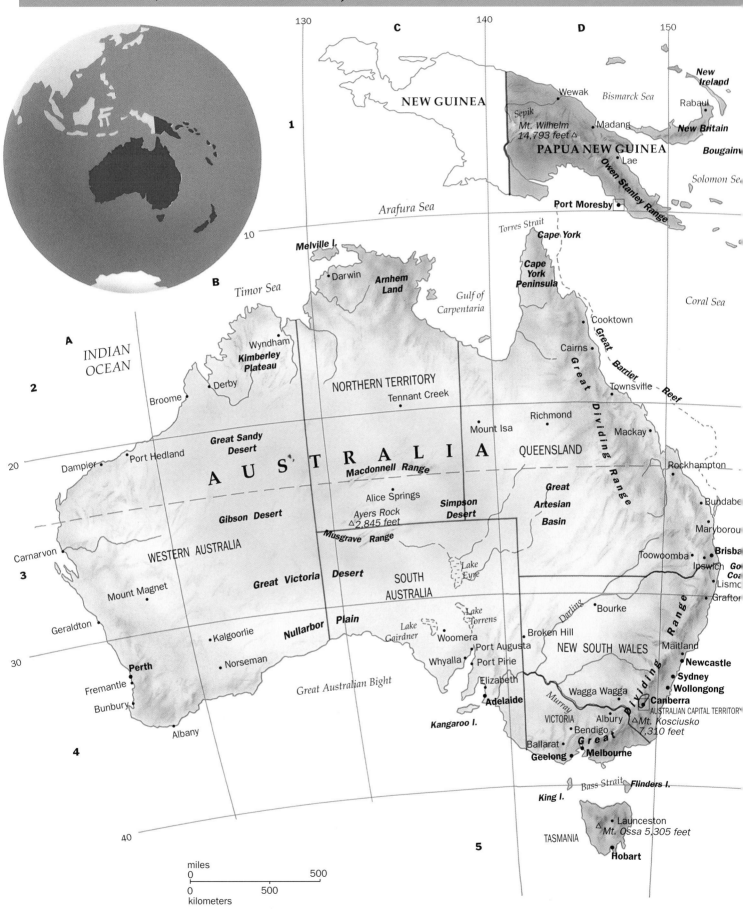

NEW GUINEA

New Ireland

Wewak ·   *Bismarck Sea*

Rabaul

Sepik   *Mt. Wilhelm* · Madang   **New Britain**

14,793 feet △

PAPUA NEW GUINEA

· Lae   ***Bougainv***

Solomon Se

Arafura Sea

Port Moresby ·

Torres Strait   **Cape York**

Melville I.   **Cape York Peninsula**

Coral Sea

· Darwin   **Arnhem Land**   *Gulf of Carpentaria*   Cooktown ·

B   *Timor Sea*

A   INDIAN OCEAN

Wyndham ·   **Kimberley Plateau**   Cairns ·

· Derby   **NORTHERN TERRITORY**   Townsville ·

Broome ·   Tennant Creek ·

Richmond ·

Mackay ·

Dampier · · Port Hedland   **Great Sandy Desert**   Mount Isa ·   **QUEENSLAND**

A U S T R A L I A   **Macdonnell Range**   Rockhampton ·

Carnarvon ·   **Gibson Desert**   Alice Springs ·   **Simpson Desert**   **Great Artesian Basin**   · Bundabe

Ayers Rock △2,845 feet   Maryborou

WESTERN AUSTRALIA   **Musgrave Range**   Toowoomba ·   **Brisba**

Mount Magnet ·   **Great Victoria Desert**   **SOUTH AUSTRALIA**   *Lake Eyre*   Ipswich   **Go Coa**

Lismc

Geraldton ·   *Lake Torrens*   *Darling*   Grafton

Kalgoorlie ·   **Nullarbor Plain**   *Lake Gairdner*   Woomera ·   · Bourke   Maitland

· Norseman   Whyalla · · Port Augusta   · Broken Hill   **NEW SOUTH WALES**   **Newcastle**

Perth   · Port Pirie   **Sydney**

Fremantle ·   Elizabeth ·   Wagga Wagga ·   **Wollongong**

Bunbury ·   *Great Australian Bight*   **Adelaide**   *Murray*   **Canberra**

AUSTRALIAN CAPITAL TERRITORY

· Albany   **VICTORIA**   Albury ·   △*Mt. Kosciusko 7,310 feet*

Kangaroo I.   · Bendigo

Ballarat ·   **Great**

Geelong · **Melbourne**

Bass Strait   **Flinders I.**

King I.

· Launceston △

TASMANIA   *Mt. Ossa 5,305 feet*

Hobart

miles
0 ————————— 500
0 ———— 500
kilometers

80

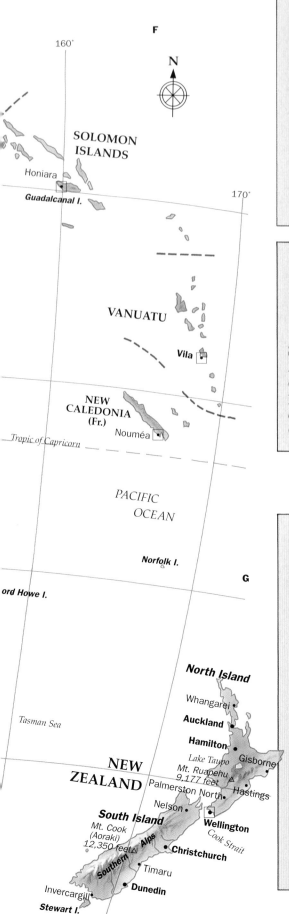

160°

N

SOLOMON
ISLANDS

Honiara

Guadalcanal I.

170°

VANUATU

Vila

NEW
CALEDONIA
(Fr.)

Nouméa

Tropic of Capricorn

PACIFIC
OCEAN

Norfolk I.

G

ord Howe I.

Tasman Sea

North Island

Whangarei

Auckland

Hamilton

NEW
ZEALAND

Lake Taupo
Mt. Ruapehu
9,177 feet

Gisborne

Palmerston North

Hastings

Nelson

South Island

Mt. Cook
(Aoraki)
12,350 feet

Southern Alps

Wellington

Cook Strait

Christchurch

Timaru

Invercargill

Dunedin

Stewart I.

PAPUA NEW GUINEA
Area: 178,703 sq miles
(461,693 sq km)
Highest point: Mount Wilhelm
14,799 ft (4,509 m)
Population: 5,420,280
Capital and largest city: Port
Moresby (pop 275,000)

VANUATU
Area: 4,710 sq miles
(12,199 sq km)
Population: 202,609
Capital: Vila (pop 34,000)

SOLOMON ISLANDS
Area: 10,985 sq miles
(28,451 sq km)
Population: 523,617
Capital and largest city: Honiara
(pop 56,000)

AUSTRALIA
Area: 2,967,908 sq miles
(7,686,882 sq km)
Highest point: Mt. Kosciusko
7,310 ft (2,220 m)
Population: 19,913,144
Capital: Canberra (pop 373,000)
Other large cities:
Sydney (4,099,000),
Melbourne (3,447,000),
Brisbane (1,626,000)
Official language: English
Religion: Christianity (76%)
Economy: *Agriculture:* wool, meat,
wheat, fruit, sugar; *Mining:* coal,
bauxite, iron ore, copper, oil,
uranium; *Industry:* machinery and
transportation equipment, foods,
chemicals, iron, paper, textiles
Currency: Australian Dollar
Government: Democratic federal
state system

NEW ZEALAND
Area: 103,738 sq miles
(268,681 sq km)
Population: 3,993,817
Capital: Wellington (pop 343,000)
Other large cities:
Auckland (1,063,000),
Christchurch (331,443)
Official language: English and Maori
Religion: Christianity (67%)
Economy: *Agriculture:* wool, meat,
dairy products; *Mining:* natural
gas, iron ore, coal; *Industry:* foods,
wood and paper, textiles
Currency: New Zealand Dollar
Government: Parlimentary
democracy

NEW CALEDONIA
(FRANCE)
Area: 7,359 sq miles
(19,060 sq km)
Population: 213,679
Capital: Nouméa (pop 76,293)

81

Pacific Ocean

Bering Sea

Gulf of Alaska

Aleutian Is.

ASIA

NORTH   PACIFIC   OCEAN

Guadalupe (Mex.

Midway Is. (U.S.)

Tropic of Cancer

Hawaiian Is. (U.S.)

Johnston I. (U.S.)

International Date Line

Northern Mariana Is.

Guam (U.S.)

Marianas Trench 35,840 feet

MARSHALL IS.

Caroline Is.

Kiritimati I.

FEDERATED STATES OF MICRONESIA

Equator

REPUBLIC OF PALAU

Gilbert Is.

Line Is.

NAURU

KIRIBATI

PAPUA NEW GUINEA

Phoenix Is.

Marquesas Is.

SOLOMON ISLANDS

Ellice Is.

Santa Cruz Is.

TUVALU

American Samoa

Tuamotu Archipelago

Wallis & Futuna (Fr.)

SAMOA

Society Is.

VANUATU

Cook Is. (N.Z.)

French Polynesia

Coral Sea

FIJI ISLANDS

TONGA

New Caledonia (Fr.)

Pitcairn I. (U.

AUSTRALIA

Norfolk Is. (Aus.)

Kermadec Is. (N.Z.)

SOUTH   PACIFIC   OCEAN

Tasman Sea

NEW ZEALAND

Chatham Is. (N.Z.)

Bounty Is. (N.Z.)

Auckland Is. (N.Z.)

Macquarie I. (Aus.)

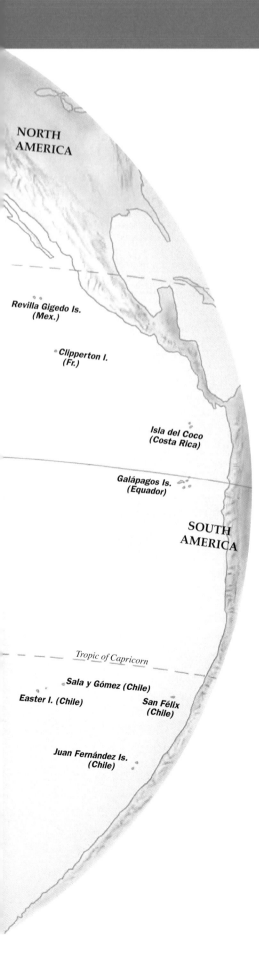

NORTH
AMERICA

Revilla Gigedo Is.
(Mex.)

Clipperton I.
(Fr.)

Isla del Coco
(Costa Rica)

Galápagos Is.
(Equador)

SOUTH
AMERICA

Tropic of Capricorn

Sala y Gómez (Chile)

Easter I. (Chile)   San Félix
(Chile)

Juan Fernández Is.
(Chile)

PACIFIC OCEAN
Area: 64,186,300 sq miles
(181,000,000 sq km)

Deepest point:
35,840 ft (10,924 m)
in the Marianas Trench

REPUBLIC OF PALAU
Area: 188 sq miles (458 sq km)
Population: 20,016
Capital: Koror (pop 14,000)

FEDERATED STATES OF MICRONESIA
Area: 271 sq miles (702 sq km)
Population: 108,155
Capital: Palikir (pop 7,000)

MARSHALL ISLANDS
Area: 70 sq miles (181 sq km)
Population: 57,728
Capital: Majuro (pop 25,000)

NAURU
Area: 8 sq miles (21 sq km)
Population: 12,809

KIRIBATI
Area: 313 sq miles (811 sq km)
Population: 100,798
Capital: South Tarawa (pop 42,000)

International Date Line
The international date line runs
north-south through the central
Pacific Ocean. When crossing the
line from east to west, travelers
lose one day. When crossing from
west to east, they gain a day.

This is because there is a 24-hour
difference between the time on
either side of the line. The line does
not follow longitude 180 degrees
exactly. It bends around islands to
avoid confusion.

TUVALU
Area: 10 sq miles (26 sq km)
Population: 11,468
Capital: Funafuti (pop 6,000)

SAMOA
Area: 1,137 sq miles (2,945 sq km)
Population: 177,714
Capital: Apia (pop 40,000)

FIJI ISLANDS
Area: 7,054 sq miles
(18,270 sq km)
Population: 880,874
Capital: Suva (pop 210,000)

TONGA
Area: 289 sq miles (749 sq km)
Population: 110,237
Capital: Nuku'alofa (pop 35,000)

Atlantic Ocean

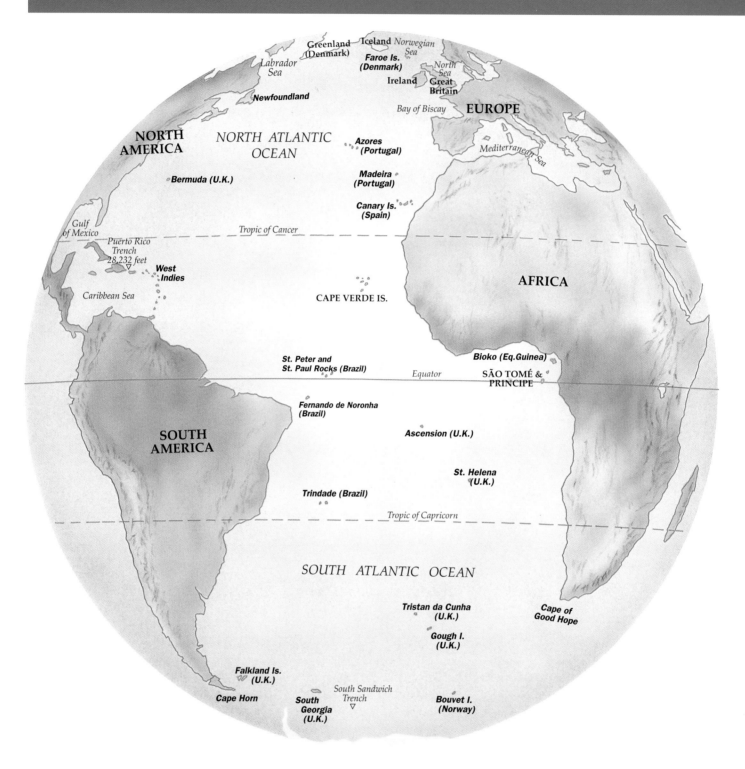

Greenland (Denmark)
Iceland
Norwegian Sea
Labrador Sea
Faroe Is. (Denmark)
North Sea
Ireland
Great Britain
Newfoundland
Bay of Biscay
EUROPE

NORTH AMERICA
NORTH ATLANTIC OCEAN
Azores (Portugal)
Mediterranean Sea

Bermuda (U.K.)
Madeira (Portugal)

Canary Is. (Spain)

Gulf of Mexico
Tropic of Cancer

Puerto Rico Trench 28,232 feet
West Indies
AFRICA

Caribbean Sea
CAPE VERDE IS.

St. Peter and St. Paul Rocks (Brazil)
Bioko (Eq.Guinea)
Equator
SÃO TOMÉ & PRINCIPE

Fernando de Noronha (Brazil)

SOUTH AMERICA
Ascension (U.K.)

St. Helena (U.K.)

Trindade (Brazil)
Tropic of Capricorn

SOUTH ATLANTIC OCEAN

Tristan da Cunha (U.K.)
Cape of Good Hope

Gough I. (U.K.)

Falkland Is. (U.K.)
South Sandwich Trench
Cape Horn
South Georgia (U.K.)
Bouvet I. (Norway)

ATLANTIC OCEAN
Area: 33,420,000 sq miles
(86,557,800 sq km)
Deepest point: 28,232 ft (8,605 m)
in the Puerto Rico Trench

INDIAN OCEAN
Area: 28,350,500 sq miles
(73,427,795 sq km)
Deepest point: 23,376 ft (7,125 m)
in the Java Trench

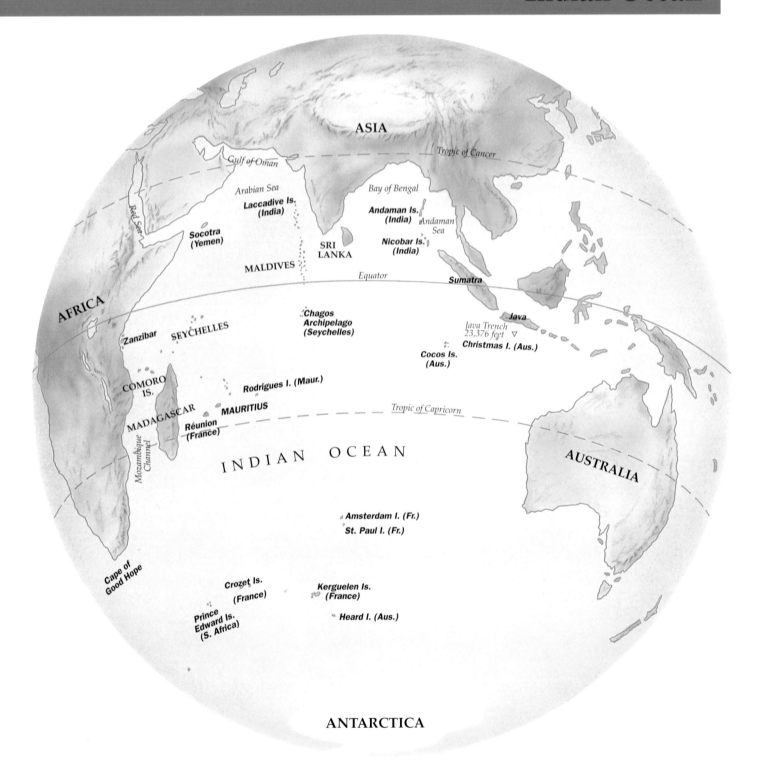

ASIA

Gulf of Oman

Tropic of Cancer

Arabian Sea

Bay of Bengal

**Laccadive Is.
(India)**

**Andaman Is.
(India)**

*Andaman
Sea*

**Socotra
(Yemen)**

SRI
LANKA

**Nicobar Is.
(India)**

MALDIVES

Red Sea

AFRICA

Equator

Sumatra

**Chagos
Archipelago
(Seychelles)**

*Java Trench
23,376 feet* ▽

Java

Zanzibar SEYCHELLES

Christmas I. (Aus.)

**Cocos Is.
(Aus.)**

**COMORO
IS.**

Rodrigues I. (Maur.)

MADAGASCAR

MAURITIUS

Tropic of Capricorn

**Réunion
(France)**

*Mozambique
Channel*

AUSTRALIA

I N D I A N   O C E A N

**Cape of
Good Hope**

Amsterdam I. (Fr.)

St. Paul I. (Fr.)

**Crozet Is.
(France)**

**Kerguelen Is.
(France)**

**Prince
Edward Is.
(S. Africa)**

Heard I. (Aus.)

ANTARCTICA

MALDIVES
Area: 116 sq miles (300 sq km)
Population: 339,330
Capital: Male (pop 83,000)

SEYCHELLES
Area: 176 sq miles (456 sq km)
Population: 80,832
Capital: Victoria (pop 25,000)

MAURITIUS
Area: 788 sq miles (2,041 sq km)
Population: 1,220,481
Capital: Port Louis (pop 143,000)

Arctic Ocean

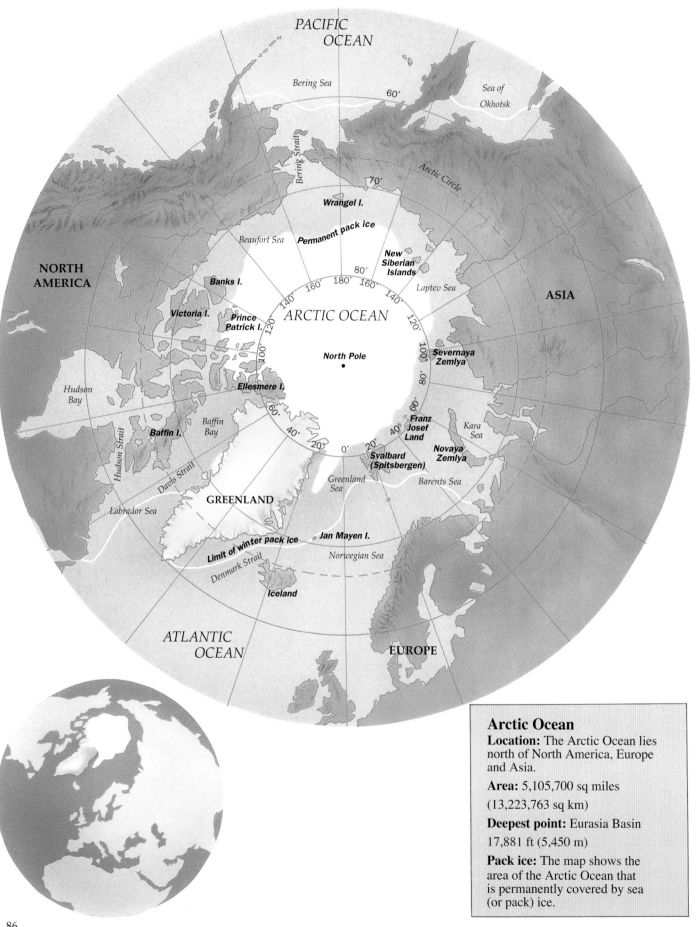

PACIFIC OCEAN

Bering Sea

Sea of Okhotsk

60°

Arctic Circle

70°

Wrangel I.

Beaufort Sea

Permanent pack ice

New Siberian Islands

Laptev Sea

80°

160° 180° 160°

140° 140°

ASIA

Banks I.

120° 120°

Victoria I.

Prince Patrick I.

ARCTIC OCEAN

100° 100°

Severnaya Zemlya

North Pole

.08

NORTH AMERICA

Ellesmere I.

60°

Hudson Bay

Franz Josef Land

Kara Sea

40° 40°

Baffin Bay

Baffin I.

20° 20°

Novaya Zemlya

Davis Strait

0°

Svalbard (Spitsbergen)

Hudson Strait

Greenland Sea

Barents Sea

Labrador Sea

GREENLAND

Jan Mayen I.

Limit of winter pack ice

Norwegian Sea

Denmark Strait

Iceland

ATLANTIC OCEAN

EUROPE

Arctic Ocean

Location: The Arctic Ocean lies north of North America, Europe and Asia.

Area: 5,105,700 sq miles (13,223,763 sq km)

Deepest point: Eurasia Basin 17,881 ft (5,450 m)

Pack ice: The map shows the area of the Arctic Ocean that is permanently covered by sea (or pack) ice.

Antarctica

Location: Antarctica is a frozen continent at the South Pole. The waters around Antarctica are sometimes called the Southern Ocean, but many geographers still consider these waters to be part of the Pacific, Atlantic, and Indian oceans.

Area: About 5,405,428 sq miles (about 13,997,468 sq km)

Population: None permanent

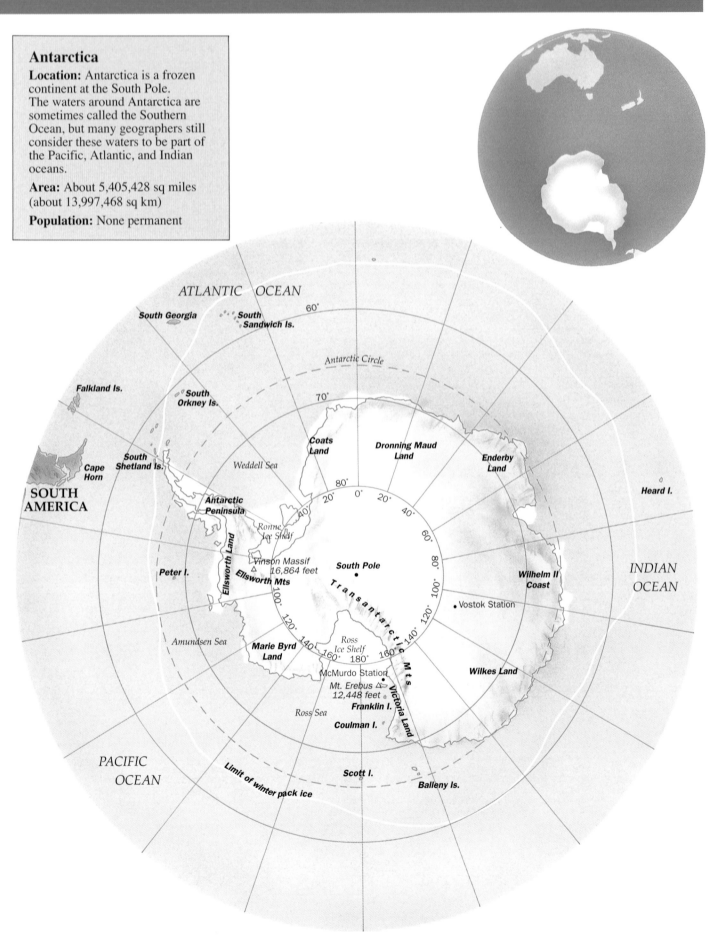

ATLANTIC OCEAN

South Georgia
South Sandwich Is.
60°

Antarctic Circle

Falkland Is.
South Orkney Is.
70°

Coats Land
Dronning Maud Land
Enderby Land

Cape Horn
South Shetland Is.
Weddell Sea
80°

SOUTH AMERICA

Antarctic Peninsula
Ronne Ice Shelf
40°
20° 0° 20°
40°

Heard I.

Ellsworth Land
Vinson Massif △ 16,864 feet
Ellsworth Mts
60°

Peter I.
100°
South Pole
80°

Wilhelm II Coast

INDIAN OCEAN

Transantarctic Mts

Vostok Station

120°
Amundsen Sea
Marie Byrd Land
140°
Ross Ice Shelf
160° 180° 160°

120°
140°

Wilkes Land

McMurdo Station
Mt. Erebus △ 12,448 feet
Franklin I.
Ross Sea
Coulman I.

Victoria Land

PACIFIC OCEAN

Limit of winter pack ice
Scott I.
Balleny Is.

Index

Goteborg 48 F5
Gotland 48 G5
Gough I. 84
Governador Valadares 36 E4
Grafton 80 E3
Grampian Mts. 45 E2
Granada (Nicaragua) 31 G5
Granada (Spain) 46 D4
Gran Canaria 46 J6
Gran Chaco 37 C5
Grand Bahama I. 32 B1
Grand Canyon 29 E3
Grand Coulee Dam 29 D1
Grand Forks 26 B1
Grand Island 26 B2
Grand Junction 29 F3
Grand Rapids 27 D2
Grand Turk 33 C2
Grantham 45 F4
Granville 42 C2
Graz 50 D3
Great Abaco I. 32 B1
Great Artesian Basin 80 D3
Great Australian Bight 80 B4
Great Barrier Reef 80 D2
Great Basin 29 D3
Great Bear L. 18 B2
Great Bend 26 B3
Great Dividing Range 80 D4
Greater Antilles 32 B3
Great Exuma I. 32 B2
Great Falls 29 E1
Great Inagua I. 33 C2
Great Karroo 76 B3
Great Ouse R. 45 G4
Great Plains 29 F1
Great Rift Valley 71 F4
Great Salt Lake 29 E2
Great Sandy Desert 80 B3
Great Slave Lake 18 B2
Great Victoria Desert 80 B3
Great Wall of China 64 D2
Great Yarmouth 45 G4
Greece 53 E3
Greeley 29 G2
Green Bay 27 D2
Greenland 19 E2
Greenland Sea 86
Greenock 45 D3
Greensboro 25 G1
Greenville (MS) 24 D2
Greenville (SC) 25 F2
Grenada 33 E4
Grenoble 43 F4
Gretna Green 45 E3
Grimsby 45 F4
Groningen 50 B1
Gross Glockner 50 C3
Grozny 54 B2
Guadalajara (Mexico) 30 D3
Guadalajara (Spain) 47 D2
Guadalcanal I. 81 F1
Guadalquivir R. 46 C4
Guadalupe I. 82
Guadalupe Peak 24 B2
Guadeloupe 33 E3
Guadiana R, 46 C3
Guam 82
Guanabacoa 32 A2
Guane 32 A2
Guangzhou 65 D3
Guantanamo 32 B2
Guasave 30 C2
Guatemala 31 F4
Guatemala City 31 F5
Guaviare R. 36 C2
Guayaquil 36 B3
Guernsey 45 H5
Guiana Highlands 36 C2
Guildford 45 F5
Guilin 64 D3

Guinea 72 D4
Guinea-Bissau 72 D4
Guines 32 A2
Guiyang 64 C3
Gujranwala 63 C2
Gulf, The 60 D3
Gulfport 25 E2
Gulu 75 C1
Gunnbjorn, Mt 19 F2
Guntur 63 E5
Gusau 73 H4
Guwahati 63 G3
Guyana 36 D2
Gwadar 62 A3
Gwalior 63 D3
Gweru 76 B2
Gyandzha 54 B2
Gyor 50 D3

H
Haarlem 50 A1
Hadejia R. 73 I4
Hadhramaut 60 C5
Hafar 60 C3
Hafnarfjordhur 48 A2
Hagerstown 23 E4
Hague, The 50 A1
Haifa 59 C3
Haikou 64 D4
Hail 60 B3
Hainan 64 D4
Haiphong 66 B1
Haiti 33 C3
Hakodate 65 F2
Halberstadt 50 C2
Halifax (Canada) 19 D3
Halifax (U.K.) 45 F4
Halle 50 C2
Halmahera 67 D3
Halmstad 48 F5
Hama 59 D3
Hamadan 60 C2
Hamar 48 E4
Hamburg 50 C1
Hameenlinna 48 I4
Hamhung 65 E2
Hamilton (Canada) 19 D3
Hamilton (N.Z.) 81 G4
Hamilton (OH) 27 E3
Hamilton (U.K.) 45 D3
Hammerfest 48 H1
Hampton 23 F5
Handan 65 D2
Hangzhou 65 E3
Hanoi 66 B1
Hanover 50 B1
Haradh 60 C4
Harar 71 G4
Harare 76 C2
Harbin 65 E1
Hardanger Plateau 48 D4
Hargeisa 71 G4
Hamosand 48 G3
Harrisburg 23 E3
Harrison 24 D1
Harrisonburg 23 E4
Harrogate 45 F4
Harstad 48 G2
Hartford 23 G3
Hartlepool 45 F3
Harz Mts. 50 C2
Hasselt 43 F1
Hastings (NE) 26 B2
Hastings (N.Z.) 81 G4
Hastings (U.K.) 45 G5
Hat Yai 66 B3
Hatteras, Cape 25 G1
Hattiesburg 25 E2
Haugesund 48 D4
Havana 32 A2
Havre 29 F1
Hawaii 28 A1

Hawaiian Is. 82
Hawick 45 E3
Hays 26 B3
Heard I. 85
Hebron 59 C4
Hefei 65 D3
Heidelberg 50 B2
Heilbronn 50 B2
Heimaey I. 48 A2
Hejaz 60 A4
Helena 29 E1
Helsingborg 48 F5
Helsinki 48 I4
Hengyang 65 D3
Herat 62 A2
Hereford 45 E4
Hermosillo 30 B2
Herning 48 E5
Hidalgo del Parral 30 C2
Hierro 46 I6
High Atlas Mts. 70 B1
High Point 25 G1
Hilo 28 A1
Himalayas 63 D2, 64 B3
Hindu Kush 62 B2
Hinggan Range, Greater 65 D1
Hinggan Range, Lesser 65 E1
Hiroshima 65 F2
Ho 73 G5
Hobart 80 D5
Ho Chi Minh City 66 B2
Hodmezovasarhely 51 E3
Hofn 48 C2
Hohhot 65 D2
Hokkaido 65 F2
Holguin 32 B2
Holon 59 C3
Holstebro 48 E5
Holyhead 45 D4
Holy I. 45 F3
Honduras 31 G5
Honduras, Gulf of 31 G4
Hong Kong 65 D3
Honiara 81 E1
Honolulu 28 A1
Honshu 65 F2
Hoover Dam 29 E3
Hopkinsville 22 B5
Hormuz, Strait of 61 E3
Hospitalet 47 G2
Hot Springs 24 D2
Houston 24 C3
Hovsgol L. 64 C1
Howrah 63 F4
Hradec Kralove 50 D2
Huainan 65 D2
Huambo 74 B3
Huancayo 36 B4
Huang He 64 C2
Huangshi 65 D3
Huascaran, Mt. 36 B3
Hubli 63 D5
Huddersfield 45 F4
Hudson Bay 19 C3
Hudson R. 23 G3
Hudson Strait 19 D2
Hue 66 B2
Huelva 46 B4
Huesca 47 E1
Hull 19 D3
Humber R, 45 F4
Humboldt R. 28 D2
Hungary 51 E3
Huntington 22 D4
Huntsville 25 E2
Huron 26 B2
Huron L. 19 C3
Hutchinson 26 B3
Hvannadalshnukur, Mt. 48 B2
Hyderabad (India) 63 D5

Hyderabad (Pakistan) 62 B3

I
Iasi 53 F1
Ibadan 73 G5
Ibague 36 B2
Ibiza 47 F3
Ica 36 B4
Iceland 48 A2
Idaho 29 E2
Idaho Falls 29 E2
Ife 73 G5
Ijsselmeer 50 A1
Ikaria 53 F4
Ilebo 74 B2
Ilesha 73 G5
Ilheus 36 F4
Iligan 67 D3
Illinois 27 D3
Illinois R. 27 C2
Iloilo 67 D2
Ilorin 73 G5
Imphal 63 G4
Inari L. 49 I2
Inchon 65 E2
Independence 26 C3
India 63 D4
Indiana 27 D2
Indianapolis 27 D3
Indian Ocean 85
Indigirka R. 55 G1
Indonesia 67 C4
Indore 63 D4
Indus R. 62 B3
Inhambane 76 C2
Inn R. 50 C2
Inner Hebrides 45 C2
Innsbruck 50 C3
Inowroclaw 50 E1
International Date Line 82
International Falls 26 C1
Invercargill 81 F5
Inverness 45 D2
Ioannina 53 D3
Iona 45 C2
Ionian Sea 53 D3
Iowa 26 C2
Iowa City 27 C2
Ipoh 66 B3
Ipswich (Australia) 80 E3
Ipswich (U.K.) 45 G4
Iquique 36 B4
Iquitos 36 B3
Iran 61 D2
Irapuato 30 D3
Iraq 60 B2
Irbid 59 C3
Irbil 60 B1
Ireland, Republic of 44 C4
Irian Jaya 67 E4
Iringa 75 D2
Irish Sea 45 D4
Irkutsk 55 E2
Ironwood 27 C1
Irrawaddy R. 66 A2
Irtysh R. 54 C2
Irun 47 E1
Isafjordhur 48 A1
Ischia 52 B3
Isere R. 43 F4
Iskenderun 59 D2
Islamabad 63 C2
Islay 45 C3
Isparta 58 B2
Israel 59 C3
Istanbul 58 B1
Italy 52 B2
Ithaca 23 F3
Ivanovo 54 B2
Iwo 73 G5

Izhevsk 54 B2
Izmir 58 A2
Izmit 58 B1

J
Jabalpur 63 D4
Jackson (MS) 24 D2
Jackson (TN) 25 E1
Jacksonville (FL) 25 F2
Jacksonville (NC) 25 G2
Jacmel 33 C3
Jaen 46 D4
Jaffna 63 E7
Jaipur 63 D3
Jakarta 66 B4
Jalalabad 62 C2
Jalapa Enriquez 30 E4
Jamaica 32 B3
Jambi 66 B4
James Bay 19 C3
James R. (SD) 26 B2
James R. (VA) 23 E4
Jamestown (ND) 26 B1
Jamestown (NY) 22 E3
Jammu 63 C2
Jamnagar 62 B4
Jamshedpur 63 F4
Janesville 27 D2
Jan Mayen I. 86
Japan 65 F2
Japan, Sea of 65 F2
Japura R. 36 B3
Jardines de la Reina 32 B2
Jaroslaw 51 F2
Java 66 B4
Java Sea 67 C4
Java Trench 85
Jebel Marra, Mt. 71 E3
Jefferson City 26 C3
Jeremie 32 C3
Jerez de la Frontera 46 B4
Jersey 45 H5
Jersey City 23 G3
Jerusalem 59 C4
Jhansi 63 D3
Jiddah 60 A4
Jihlava 50 D2
Jilin 65 E2
Jinan 65 D2
Jingdezhen 65 D3
Jinja 75 C1
Jinzhou 65 E2
Jixi 65 E1
Jizan 60 B5
Joao Pessoa 36 F3
Jodhpur 63 C3
Joensuu 49 J3
Johannesburg 76 B3
John Day River 28 C1
John o'Groats 45 E1
Johnson City 25 F1
Johnstown 22 E3
Johor Baharu 66 B3
Jonesboro 24 D1
Jonkoping 48 F5
Joplin 26 C3
Jordan 59 D4
Jordan R. 59 C3
Jos Plateau 73 H4
Jostedal Glacier 48 D4
Juan Femandez Is. 37 B6
Juba 71 F4
Juiz de Fora 37 E5
Jullundur 63 D2
Junction City 26 B3
Juneau 28 B1
Jura 45 D3
Jura Mts. 43 G3
Jurua R. 36 C3
Jutland 48 E5

Izhevsk 54 B2

K
K2 Mt. 63 D1
Kabalo 74 C2
Kabul 62 B2
Kabwe 76 B1
Kaduna 73 H4
Kafue R. 76 B2
Kagoshima 65 E3
Kahoolawe 28 A1
Kaifeng 65 D2
Kainji L. 73 G4
Kajaani 49 I3
Kalahari Desert 76 B2
Kalamata 53 E4
Kalamazoo 27 D2
Kalat 62 B3
Kalemie 74 C2
Kalgoorlie 80 B4
Kalimantan 67 C4
Kaliningrad 54 A2
Kalispell 29 E1
Kalisz 50 E2
Kallavesi L. 49 I3
Kalmar 48 G5
Kamchatka Peninsula 55 G2
Kamina 74 B2
Kampala 75 C1
Kananga 74 B2
Kanazawa 65 F2
Kandahar 62 B2
Kandy 63 E7
Kangaroo I. 80 C4
Kankakee 27 D2
Kankan 72 E4
Kannapolis 25 F1
Kano 73 H4
Kanpur 63 E3
Kansas 26 B3
Kansas City (KS) 26 C3
Kansas City (MO) 26 C3
Kansas R. 26 B3
Kaolack 72 C4
Karachi 62 B4
Karakoram Range 63 D1
Kara Kum Desert 54 C3
Karaman 59 C2
Kara Sea 55 C1
Karbala 60 B2
Kariba Dam 76 B2
Kariba L. 76 B2
Karlskrona 48 F5
Karlsruhe 50 B2
Karlstad 48 F4
Karpathos 53 F4
Kars 59 E1
Kasai R. 74 B2
Kasama 76 C1
Kashan 60 D2
Kashi 64 A2
Kassala 71 F3
Kassel 50 B2
Katahdin, Mt. 23 I1
Kathmandu 63 F3
Katowice 51 E2
Katsina 73 H4
Kattegat 48 E5
Kauai 28 A1
Kavalla 53 E3
Kawasaki 65 F2
Kayes 70 A3
Kayseri 59 C2
Kazakhstan 54 C2
Kazan 54 B2
Kebnekaise, Mt. 48 G2
Kecskemet 51 E3
Keetmanshoop 76 A3
Kefallinia 53 D3
Keflavik 48 A2

91

Kelang 66 83
Kelkit R. 59 D1
Kelso 45 E3
Kemerovo 55 02
Kemi 48 I3
Kemi R.49 I2
Kemijan/i 49 I2
Kendari 67 D4
Kenema 72 05
Kenitra 70 B1
Kennewick 28 D1
Kenora 19 C3
Kenosha 27 02
Kentucky 22 B4
Kenya 75 D1
Kenya, Mt. 75 D1
Kerguelen Is. 85
Kerintji, Mt. 66 B4
Kermadec Is. 82
Kerman 61 E2
Key West 25 F3
Khabarovsk 55 F2
Khabur R. 59 E3
Khalkis 53 E3
Khania 53 E4
Kharkov 54 A2
Khartoum 71 F3
Khartoum North 71 F3
Khaskovo 53 E3
Khios 53 E3
Khon Kaen 66 82
Khorramabad 60 C2
Khorramshahr 60 C2
Khulna 63 F4
Khvoy 60 B1
Khyber Pass 63 C2
Kiel 50 C1
Kielce 51 E2
Kiev see Kyyiv
Kigali 74 C2
Kigoma 74 C2
Kikwit 74 B2
Kildare 44 C4
Kilimanjaro, Mt. 75 D2
Kilkenny 44 C4
Killamey 44 84
Kitmarnock 45 03
Kimberley 76 B3
Kimberley Plateau 80 82
Kindia 72 D4
King I. 80 D5
King's Lynn 45 G4
Kingsport 25 F1
Kingston (Canada) 19 D3
Kingston (Jamaica) 32 83
Kingston (NY) 23 G3
Kingston upon Hull 45 F4
Kingstown 33 E4
King William I. 19 C2
Kinshasa 74 B2
Kirghizia see Kyrgyzstan
Kiribati 82
Kiritimati I. 82
Kirkcaldy 45 E2
Kirkcudbright 45 D3
Kirksville 26 C2
Kirkuk 60 B1
Kirkwall 45 G2
Kirov 54 B2
Kiruna 48 H2
Kisangani 74 C1
Kisumu 75 C2
Kitakyushu 65 E2
Kitchener 19 C3
Kithira 53 E4
Kithnos 53 E4
Kitwe 76 B1
Kivu L. 74 C2
Kizd R. 59 C1
Kladno 50 D2

Klagenfurt 50 D3
Klamath Falls 28 C2
Klar R. 48 F4
Klyuchevskaya, Mt. 55 H2
Knoxville 25 F1
Kobe 65 F2
Koblenz 50 B2
Kodiak I. 28 B1
Kokkola 48 H3
Kokomo 27 D2
Kokon Selka L. 49 I4
Kolding 48 E5
Kolhapur 63 C5
Kolkata 63 F4
Kolwezi 74 C3
Kolyma Mts. 55 G1
Kolyma R. 55 G1
Komotini 53 E3
Komsomolsk 55 F2
Konstanz 43 H3
Konya 59 C2
Korce 53 D3
Korhogo 72 E5
Kortrijk 42 E1
Kos 53 F4
Kosciusko, Mt. 80 D4
Kosice 51 E2
Koszalin 50 D1
Kota 63 D3
Kota Baharu 66 B3
Kotka 49 I4
Kotlas 54 B1
Koudougou 73 F4
Kouvola 49 I4
Kragujevac 53 D2
Krak des Chevaliers 59 03
Krakow 51 E2
Kraljevo 53 D2
Krasnodar 54 A2
Krasnovodsk 54 B2
Krasnoyarsk 55 D2
Kratie 66 B2
Krefeld 50 B2
Krems 50 D2
Krishna R. 63 D5
Kristiansand 48 D4
Kristianstad 48 F5
Kroonstad 76 B3
Krugersdorp 76 B3
Kuala Lumpur 66 B3
Kuching 67 C3
Klitahya 58 B2
Kumamoto 65 E2
Kumasi 73 F5
Kunlun Mts. 64 A2
Kunming 64 C3
Kuopio 49 I3
Kurdistan 59 E2
Kurgan 54 C2
Kuria Muria Is, 61 E5
Kuril Is. 55 G2
Kursk 54 A2
Kutahya 58 B2
Kuwait 60 C3
Kuybyshev see Samara
Kwangju 65 E2
Kwekwe 76 B2
Kyle of Lochalsh 45 D2
Kyoto 65 F2
Kyrgyzstan 54 C2
Kyushu 65 E3
Kyyiv (Kiev) 54 A2
Kyzyl Kum Desert 54 C2

L
Laayoune 70 A2
Labe 72 D4
Labrador 19 D3
Labrador Sea B6
Laccadive Is. B5
La Chaux-de-Fonds 43 G3
La Coruna 46 A1

La Crosse 27 C2
Ladoga L. 54 A1
Ladysmith 76 B3
Lae 80 D1
Lafayette (IN) 27 D2
Lafayette (LA) 24 D2
Lagos 73 G5
Lahore 63 C2
Lahti 49 I4
Lake Charles 24 D2
Lake City 25 F2
Lake District 45 E3
Lake Havasu City 29 E4
Lambarene 74 A2
Lamia 53 E3
Lanai 28 A1
Lancaster (PA) 23 F3
Lancaster (U.K.) 45 E3
Land's End 45 D5
Lansing 27 E2
Lanzarote 46 K5
Lanzhou 64 C2
Laos 66 B1
La Palma 46 I5
La Paz 36 C4
Lapland 48 H2
La Plata 37 D6
Lappeenranta 49 J4
Laptev Sea 55 F1
L'Aquila 52 B2
Laramie 29 F2
Laredo 24 C3
Larisa 53 B1
Larnaca 59 C3
Larne 45 D3
La Rochelle 42 C3
La Roche-sur-Yon 42 C3
La Romana 33 D3
Las Cruces 29 F4
La Serena 37 B5
Las Palmas 46 J5
La Spezia 52 A2
Las Vegas 29 D3
Latakia 59 C3
Latvia 54 A2
Launceston 80 D5
Lausanne. 43 G3
Laval 42 C2
La Vega 33 C3
Lawrence (KS) 26 B3
Lawrence (MA) 23 H2
Lawton 24 C2
Lebanon 59 C3
Lecce 53 D3
Leech L. 26 C1
Leeds 45 F4
Leeuwarden 50 A1
Leghorn 52 B2
Legnica 50 D2
Leh 63 D2
Le Havre 42 D2
Leicester 45 F4
Leipzig 50 C2
Leiria 46 A3
Le Mans 42 D3
Lena R. 55 F1
Lens 42 E1
Leoben 50 D3
Leon (Mexico) 30 D3
Leon (Nicaragua) 31 G5
Leon (Spain) 46 C1
Le Puy 43 E4
Lerida 47 F2
Lerwick 45 H2
Les Cayes 33 C3
Leskovac 53 D2
Lesotho 76 B3
Lesser Slave Lake 18 B3
Lesvos 53 E3
Lethbridge 18 B3
Levittown 23 G3

Levkas 53 D3
Lewis 45 C1
Lewiston (ID) 29 D1
Lewiston (ME) 23 H2
Lexington 22 C4
Lexington Park 23 F4
Leyte 67 D2
Lhasa 64 B3
Lianyungang 65 D2
Liberal 26 A3
Liberec 50 D2
Liberia 72 E5
Libreville 74 A1
Libya 70 D2
Libyan Desert 71 E2
Lichinga 76 C1
Liechtenstein 43 H3
Liege 43 F1
Liffey R. 45 C4
Ligurian Sea 52 A2
Likasi 74 C3
Lille 42 E1
Lillehammer 48 E4
Lilongwe 76 C1
Lima (OH) 27 E2
Lima (Peru) 36 B4
Limassol 59 C3
Limerick 44 B4
Limnos 53 E3
Limoges 42 D4
Limpopo R. 76 B2
Linares 46 D3
Lincoln (U.K.) 45 F4
Lincoln (NE) 26 B2
Line Is. 82
Linkoping 48 F4
Linz 50 D2
Lion, Gulf of 43 F5
Lipari Is. 52 C3
Lisbon 46 A3
Lisburn 45 C3
Lishore 80 E3
Little Abaco I. 32 B1
Little Colorado R. 29 E3
Little Karroo 76 B3
Little Rock 24 D2
Liuzhou 64 D3
Livermore, Mt. 24 B2
Liverpool 45 E4
Livingstone 76 B2
Livonia 27 E2
Ljubljana 52 C1
Ljungan R. 48 F3
Llandrindod Wells 45 E4
Llandudno 45 E4
Llanelli 45 D5
Lobito 74 A3
Locarno 43 H3
Lochinver 45 D1
Loch Lomond 45 D2
Loch Ness 45 D2
Lodz 51 E2
Lofoten Is. 48 F2
Logan 29 E2
Logan Mt. I8 A2
Logrono 47 D1
Loire R. 42 D3
Lomami R. 74 B2
Lombok 67 C4
Lome 73 G5
Lomza 51 F2
London (Canada) 19 C3
London (U.K.) 45 F5
Londonderry 44 C3
Long Beach 28 D4
Long I. (Bahamas) 32 B2
Long I. (NY) 23 G3
Longview 24 D2
Lorain 27 E2
Lorca 47 E4

Lord Howe I. 81 E4
Lorient 42 B3
Los Alamos 29 F3
Los Angeles 28 D4
Los Mochis 30 C2
Lot R. 42 D4
Louisiana 24 D2
Louisville 22 B4
Lourdes 42 C5
Loveland 29 F2
Lowell 23 H2
Lower Tunguska R. 55 D1
Lowestoft 45 G4
Lualaba R. 74 C2
Luanda 74 A2
Luang Prabang 66 B2
Luangwa R. 76 C1
Lubango 74 A3
Lubbock 24 B2
Lubeck 50 C1
Lublin 51 F2
Lubumbashi 74 C3
Lucca 52 B2
Lucena 67 D2
Lucknow 63 E3
Luderitz 76 A3
Ludhiana 63 D2
Lugano 43 H3
Lugo 46 B1
Lukenie R. 74 B2
Lule R. 48 H2
Lulea 48 H3
Lund 48 F5
Lundy I. 45 D5
Luoyang 65 D2
Lurgan 45 C3
Lusaka 76 B2
Luton 45 F5
Luxembourg 43 G2
Luxor 71 F2
Luzern 43 H3
Luzhou 64 C3
Luzon 67 D2
Lviv 54 A2
Lynchburg 22 E5
Lyon 43 F4

M
Ma'an 59 C4
Maas R. 50 A2
Maastricht 50 A2
McAllen 24 C3
Macao 65 D3
McComb 24 D2
McCook 26 A2
Macdonnell Range 80 C3
Macedonia 53 D3
Maceio 36 F3
Mackay 80 D3
Mackenzie Mts. 18 A2
Mackenzie R. 18 A2
McKinley, Mt. 28 B1
McMurdo Station 87
Macon (France) 43 F3
Macon (GA) 25 F2
Macquarie I. 82
Madang 80 D1
Madagascar 77 D2
Madeira 84
Madeira R. 36 C3
Madison 27 D2
Madras see Chennai
Madrid 46 D2
Madurai 63 D7
Mafia I. 75 D2
Mafikeng 76 B3
Magadan 55 G2
Magdeburg 50 C1
Magellan, Strait of 37 C8
Maggiore L. 52 A1
Magnolia 24 D2

Mahajanga 77 D2
Mahalapye 76 B2
Mahon 47 H3
Maiduguri 73 I4
Main R. 50 C2
Maine 23 I1
Mainz 50 B2
Maitland 80 E4
Majene 67 C4
Majorca 47 G3
Makeni 72 D5
Makurdi 73 H5
Malabo 74 A1
Malaga 46 C3
Malang 67 C4
Malange 74 B2
Malatya 59 D2
Malawi 76 C1
Malawi L. 76 C1
Malaysia 66 B3
Maldives 85
Mali 70 B3
Malin Head 44 C3
Malindi 75 D2
Mallaig 45 D2
Malmo 48 F5
Malta 52 C4
Man 72 E5
Man, Isle of 45 D3
Manado 67 D3
Managua 31 G5
Manaus 36 C3
Manchester (NH) 23 H2
Manchester (U.K.) 45 E4
Manchurian Plain 65 E1
Mandalay 66 A1
Mandeville 32 B3
Mangalore 63 C6
Manhattan 26 B3
Manila 67 D2
Manisa 58 A2
Manistee 27 D2
Manitoba 19 C3
Manitoba L. 19 C3
Manitowoc 27 D2
Manizales 36 B2
Mankato 26 C2
Mannar, Gulf of 63 D7
Mannheim 50 B2
Manokwari 67 E4
Manresa 47 F2
Mansfield (OH) 27 E2
Mansfield (U.K.) 45 F4
Manta 36 A3
Manzanillo 32 B2
Maoke Range 67 E4
Maputo 76 C3
Maracaibo 36 B1
Maracay 36 C1
Maranon R. 36 B3
Maras 59 D2
Marcy, Mt. 23 G2
Mardan 63 C2
Mar del Plata 37 06
Margarita I. 36 C1
Margate 45 G5
Man 59 D3
Marianas Trench 82
Maribor 52 C1
Marie Byrd Land 87
Marietta 25 F2
Marinette 27 D1
Marion 27 E2
Maritsa R. 53 F3
Mariupol 54 A2
Marmara, Sea of 58 B1
Marne R. 42 E2
Maromokotro, Mt. 77 D1
Maroua 74 A1
Marquesas Is. 82

Orlando 25 F3
Orleans 42 D3
Omskoldsvik 48 G3
Orsk 54 B2
Orumiyeh 60 B1
Oruro 36 C4
Osaka 65 F2
Oshawa 19 D3
Oshkosh 27 D2
Oshogbo 73 G5
Osijek 53 D2
Oskaloosa 26 C2
Oslo 48 E4
Osmaniye 59 D2
Osnabruck 50 B1
Osorno 37 B7
Ossa, Mt. 80 D5
Ostend 42 E1
Ostersund 48 F3
Ostrava 50 E2
Oti R. 73 G5
Ottawa 19 D3
Ottawa R. 19 D3
Ottumwa 26 C2
Ouachita Mts. 24 D2
Ouachita R. 24 D2
Ouagadougou 73 F4
Ouahigouya 73 F4
Oujda 70 B1
Oulu 49 I3
Oulujarvi L. 49 I3
Ouse R. 45 F3
Outer Hebrides 44 C2
Oviedo 46 C1
Owensboro 22 84
Owen Stanley Range 80 D1
Oxford (MS) 25 E2
Oxford (U.K.) 45 F5
Oyo 73 G5
Ozark Plateau 26 C3

P
Paarl 76 A3
Pachuca 30 E3
Pacific Ocean 82
Padang 66 B4
Padua 52 B2
Paducah 22 A5
Paijanne L. 49 I4
Paisley 45 O3
Pakanbaru 66 B3
Pakistan 62 B3
Pakse 66 B2
Palau, Republic of 82
Palawan 67 C3
Palembang 66 B4
Palencia 46 C1
Palermo 52 B3
Palime 73 G5
Palma 47 G3
Palmerston North 81 G5
Palmyra 59 D3
Palu 67 C4
Pamir Mts. 54 C3
Pamlico Sound 25 G1
Pampa 37 C6
Pamplona 47 E1
Panama 31 H6
Panama Canal 31 I6
Panama City (FL) 25 E2
Panama City (Panama) 31 I6
Panama, Gulf of 31 I6
Panay 67 C3
Pantelleria 52 B4
Paphos 59 C3
Papua New Guinea 80 D1
Paraguay 37 D5
Paraguay R. 36 D4
Parakou 73 G5
Paramaribo 36 D2
Parana 37 C6
Parana R. 37 D5

Pardubice 50 D2
Paris (France) 42 E2
Paris (TX) 24 C2
Parkersburg 22 D4
Parma (Italy) 52 B2
Parma (OH) 27 E2
Parmaiba 36 E3
Pascagoula 25 E2
Passo Fundo 37 D5
Pasto 36 B2
Patagonia 37 C7
Paterson 23 G3
Patiala 63 D2
Patna 63 F3
Patras 53 D3
Pau 42 C5
Pavia 52 A2
Paysandu 37 D6
Peace R. 18 B3
Pearl R. 24 D2
Pec 53 D2
Pecos 24 B2
Pecos R. 24 B2
Pecs 50 E3
Peebles 45 E3
Pee Dee R. 25 G2
Pegu 66 A2
Peipus L. 54 A2
Pekalongan 66 B4
Pelotas 37 D6
Pematangsiantar 66 A3
Pemba 76 D1
Pemba I. 75 D2
Pembroke 45 D5
Pendleton 28 D1
Pennines 45 E3
Pennsylvania 23 F3
Penrith 45 E3
Pensacola 25 E2
Penza 54 B2
Penzance 45 D5
Peoria 27 D2
Pereira 36 B2
Perigueux 42 D4
Perm 54 B2
Pernik 53 E2
Perpignan 42 E5
Perth (Australia) 80 A4
Perth (Scotland) 45 E2
Peru 36 B3
Perugia 52 B2
Pescara 52 C2
Peshawar 63 C2
Peterborough (Canada) 19 D3
Peterborough (England) 45 F4
Peterhead 45 F2
Peter I. 87
Petersburg 23 F5
Petra 59 C4
Petropavlosk-Kamchatskiy 55 G2
Petrozavodsk 54 A1
Phenix City 25 E2
Philadelphia 23 F3
Philippines 67 D2
Phitsanulok 66 B2
Phnom Penh 66 B2
Phoenix 29 E4
Phoenix Is. 82
Phuket 66 A3
Piacenza 52 A2
Piatra Neamt 53 F1
Piedras Negras 30 D2
Pielinen L. 49 J3
Pierre 26 A2
Pietermaritzburg 76 C3
Pietersburg 76 B2
Pila 50 D1
Pilcomayo R. 37 C5
Pinar del Rio 32 A2
Pindus Mts. 53 D3
Pine Bluff 24 D2

Pine Ridge 26 A2
Pinios R. 53 E3
Piotrkow 51 E2
Piraeus 53 E4
Pisa 52 B2
Pitcairn I. 82
Pitesti 53 E2
Pittsburgh 22 E3
Pittsfield 23 G3
Piura 36 A3
Plasencia 46 B2
Platte R. 26 B2
Plattsburgh 23 G2
Plauen 50 C2
Pleven 53 E2
Plock 51 E1
Ploesti 53 F2
Plovdiv 53 E2
Plymouth (Montserrat) 33 E3
Plymouth (U.K.) 45 D5
Plzert 50 C2
Pocatello 29 E2
Podgorica 53 D2
Pointe Noire 74 A2
Poitiers 42 D3
Pokhara 63 E3
Poland 51 E2
Ponca City 24 C1
Ponce 33 D3
Ponferrada 46 B1
Ponta Grossa 37 D5
Pontchartrain L. 24 D2
Pontevedra 46 A1
Pontiac 27 E2
Pontianak 66 B4
Poole 45 F5
Poopo L. 36 C4
Popayan 36 B3
Poplar Bluff 27 C3
Popocatepetl Volcano 30 E4
Po R. 52 B2
Pori 48 H4
Portadown 45 C3
Port Arthur 24 D3
Port Augusta 80 C4
Port Bou 47 G1
Port Elizabeth 76 B3
Port Gentil 74 A2
Port Harcourt 73 H6
Port Hedland 80 A3
Portland (ME) 23 H2
Portland (OR) 28 C1
Port Laoise 44 C4
Port Moresby 80 D1
Porto 46 A2
Porto Alegre 37 D6
Port of Spain 33 E4
Porto-Novo 73 G5
Porto Velho 36 C3
Port Pirie 80 C4
Port Said 71 F1
Portsmouth (NH) 23 H2
Portsmouth (OH) 27 E3
Portsmouth (U.K.) 45 F5
Portsmouth (VA) 23 F5
Port Sudan 71 F3
Port Talbot 45 E5
Portugal 46 A3
Posadas 37 D5
Potchefstroom 76 B3
Potenza 52 C3
Potomac R. 23 E4
Potosi 36 C4
Potsdam 50 C1
Poughkeepsie 23 G3
Powder R. 29 F1
Powell L. 29 E3
Poznan 50 D1
Prague 50 D2
Praia 72 B2

Prato 52 B2
Prescott 29 E4
Presidente Prudente 37 D5
Presque Isle 23 I1
Preston 45 E4
Pretoria 76 B3
Pribram 50 D2
Prijedor 53 C2
Prince Albert 18 B3
Prince Edward 1.19 D3
Prince Edward Is. 85
Prince George 18 A3
Prince of Wales 1.19 C2
Prince Patrick I. 86
Prince Rupert 18 A3
Pristina 53 D2
Providence 23 H3
Provideniya 55 I1
Provo 29 E2
Prut R. 53 F1
Przemysl 51 F2
Pucallpa 36 B3
Puebla 30 E4
Pueblo 29 G3
Puerto de Santa Maria 46 B4
Puertollano 46 C3
Puerto Montt 37 B7
Puerto Plata 33 C3
Puerto Rico 33 D3
Puerto Rico Trench 84
Pula 52 B2
Pulawy 51 E2
Puncak Jaya 67 E4
Pune 63 C5
Punta Arenas 37 B8
Purus R. 36 C3
Pusan 65 E2
Putumayo R. 36 B3
Pyongyang 65 E2
Pyrenees 42 D5

Q
Qaraghandy 54 C2
Qatar 60 D3
Qattara Depression 71 E2
Qazvin 60 D1
Qena 71 F2
Qilian Mts. 64 C2
Qingdao 65 E2
Qinghai L. 64 C2
Qiqihar 65 E1
Qom 60 D2
Qonduz 62 B1
Quebec 19 D3
Queen Charlotte Is. 18 A3
Queensland 80 D3
Queenstown 76 B3
Quelimane 76 C2
Queretaro 30 D3
Quetta 62 B2
Qui Nhon 66 B2
Quincy 27 C2
Quito 36 B3
Qyzylorda 54 C2

R
Rabat 70 B1
Rabaul 80 E1
Rach Gia 66 B2
Racine 27 D2
Radom 51 E2
Ragged I. 32 C2
Ragusa 52 C4
Rainier. Mt. 28 C1
Rainy L. 26 C1
Raipur 63 E4
Rajahmundry 63 E5
Rajkot 62 C4
Rajshahi 63 F4
Raleigh 25 G1
Ramat Gan 59 C3
Rancagua 37 B6

Ranchi 63 F4
Randers 48 E5
Rapid City 26 A2
Rasht 60 C1
Rauma 48 H4
Ravenna 52 B2
Ravensburg 50 B3
Rawalpindi 63 C2
Rawlins 29 F2
Razgrad 53 F2
Re, lie de 42 C3
Reading (PA) 23 F3
Reading (U.K.) 45 F5
Recife 36 E3
Red Deer 18 B3
Red Lakes 26 C1
Red R. (U.S.) 24 D2
Red R. (Vietnam) 66 B1
Red Sea 71 F2
Red Volta R. 73 F4
Regensburg 50 C2
Reggio di Calabria 52 C3
Reggio nell'Emilia 52 B2
Regina 18 B3
Reims 43 F2
Rennes 42 C2
Reno 28 D3
Republican R, 26 B2
Resistencia 37 D5
Resita 53 E2
Reunion 85
Reus 47 F2
Reykjavik 48 A2
Reynosa 30 E2
Rhine R. 50 B2
Rhode Island 23 H3
Rhodes 53 F4
Rhodope Mts. 53 E3
Rhone R. 43 F4
Rhum 45 C2
Ribeirao Preto 37 E5
Richmond (Australia) 80 D3
Richmond (VA) 23 F4
Rift Valley 75 C1
Riga 54 A2
Rigestan Desert 62 A2
Rijeka 52 C2
Rimini 52 B2
Ringerike 48 E4
Riobamba 36 B3
Rio Bravo del Norte see Rio Grande
Rio Cuarto 37 C6
Rio de Janeiro 37 E5
Rio Grande 24 A2, 30 D2
Rivera 37 D6
Riyadh 60 C4
Rize 59 E1
Road Town 33 E3
Roanne 43 F3
Roanoke 22 E5
Robson, Mt. 18 B3
Rochester (MN) 26 C2
Rochester (NH) 23 H2
Rochester (NY) 23 H2
Rockford 27 D2
Rockhampton 80 E3
Rock Hill 25 F2
Rock I. 27 C2
Rock R. 27 D2
Rock Springs 29 F2
Rocky Mount 25 G1
Rocky Mts. 18 A3, 29 E2
Rodez 42 E4
Rodrigues Is. 85
Roeselare 42 E1
Rogers, Mt. 22 D5
Rolla 27 C3
Romania 53 E2
Rome (GA) 25 E2
Rome (Italy) 52 B3

Rosa, Mt. 52 A2
Rosario 37 C6
Roscommon 44 B4
Roscrea 44 C4
Roseau 33 E3
Roseau 33 E3
Rosslare 45 C4
Ross Sea 87
Rostock 50 C1
Rostov 54 A2
Roswell 29 G4
Rotherham 45 F4
Rotterdam 50 A2
Rouen 42 D2
Rovaniemi 49 I2
Ruapehu, Mt. 81 G4
Rub al Khali 7, 60 C5
Rugby 26 B1
Rukwa L. 75 C2
Rum Cay 32 C2
Rundu 76 A1
Russian Federation 54 B2
Ruston 24 D2
Rutland 23 G2
Ruvuma R, 76 C1
Ruwenzori Range 75 C1
Rwanda 75 C2
Ryazan 54 A2
Ryukyu Is. 65 E3
Rzeszow 51 E2

S
Saarbrucken 50 B2
Sabadell 47 G2
Sabah 67 C3
Sable, Cape 19 D3
Sacramento 28 C3
Sacramento R. 28 C3
Safi 70 B1
Sagar 63 D4
Saginaw 27 E2
Sagunto 47 E3
Sahara 70 C2
Saharanpur 63 D3
Sahel 70 C3
Saidpur 63 F3
St. Albans 45 F5
St. Andrews 45 E2
St. Austell 45 D5
St-Brieuc 42 B2
St. Cloud 26 C1
St. Croix R. 26 C1
St-Denis 42 E2
St-Die 43 G2
St-Dizier 43 F2
St-Etienne 43 F4
St. Gallon 43 H3
St. George's 33 E4
St. George's Channel 45 D4
St. Helena 84
St. Helens, Mt. 28 C1
St. Holier 45 H5
Saint John 19 D3
St. John's (Antigua) 33 E3
St. John's (Canada) 19 E3
St. Joseph 26 C3
St. Kilda 44 B2
St. Kitts Nevis 33 E3
St. Lawrence R. 19 D3
St. Louis (MO) 27 C3
St. Louis (Senegal) 72 C3
St. Lucia 33 E4
St-Malo 42 C2
St. Marc 33 C3
St. Martin 33 E3
St. Moritz 43 H3
St- Nazaire 42 B3
St. Paul 26 C2
St. Paul I. 85
St. Peter & St. Paul Rocks 84
St. Peter Port 45 H5